BRIGHT

A SEPARATE PEACE
BY
JOHN KNOWLES

Intelligent Education

INFLUENCE PUBLISHERS

Nashville, Tennessee

BRIGHT NOTES: A Separate Peace

www.BrightNotes.com

No part of this publication may be used or reproduced in any manner whatsoever without written permission, except in the case of brief quotations in critical articles and reviews. For permissions, contact Influence Publishers http://www.influencepublishers.com.

ISBN: 978-1-645422-72-3 (Paperback)
ISBN: 978-1-645422-73-0 (eBook)

Published in accordance with the U.S. Copyright Office Orphan Works and Mass Digitization report of the register of copyrights, June 2015.

Originally published by Monarch Press.
Christopher Russell Reaske, 1966
2020 Edition published by Influence Publishers.

Interior design by Lapiz Digital Services. Cover Design by Thinkpen Designs.

Printed in the United States of America.

Library of Congress Cataloging-in-Publication Data forthcoming.
Names: Intelligent Education
Title: BRIGHT NOTES: A Separate Peace
Subject: STU004000 STUDY AIDS / Book Notes

CONTENTS

1) Introduction to John Knowles   1

2) Textual Analysis   7
     Chapters 1 - 4   7
     Chapters 5 - 7   27
     Chapters 8 - 10   40
     Chapters 11 - 13   56

3) Character Analyses   73

4) Critical Commentary   80

5) Essay Questions and Answers   83

6) Bibliography   90

JOHN KNOWLES

. . . .

A WAR NOVEL

John Knowles' *A Separate Peace* is an intensive inquiry into the nature of war. It is the story of how a group of sixteen-year-old boys, all students at Devon, an American preparatory school, attempts to establish a peace far away from the war in the large outside world. Each boy, in a different way, views the war as a disaster which will sweep them all away unless it can be resisted. Each student, as he nears eligibility for the draft, confronts the facts about war in a different way. While Knowles never takes us into real war, in the sense of combat, he leads us into the war through the ways in which war is viewed by maturing adolescents on the brink of being called to do their part. Thus *A Separate Peace* is, first and foremost, a war novel. But because the action takes place far away from the war, it is a very unusual war novel.

MAINSPRING OF WAR

Knowles' conclusion about the cause of war is presented through the thinking of the narrator, Gene Forrester. In attempting to enjoy a "separate peace" at Devon the boys, in fact, engage in warlike activities. They are unable to escape from the concept of war merely because they are removed from the battlefield. As human beings they are all potential warriors. Men everywhere share one supreme defect, a tendency to make war. The nature of the enemy changes but the nature of the warring instinct does not. As Gene states four pages from the end of the novel, "it seemed clear that wars were not made by generations and their special stupidities, but that wars were made instead by something ignorant in the human heart." Because of this basic human ignorance, war will always exist in one form or another, if not on actual battlefields, on school playgrounds, and in the minds and hearts of individuals everywhere. This tendency is not so much to be pitied as simply to be recognized. Although some of the boys at Devon can, with varying success, ignore the reality of war temporarily, sooner or later this reality will come crushingly in upon them. War will intrude into private "separate" peaces everywhere.

POINT OF VIEW

The novel is narrated by Gene Forrester. Knowles is, in effect, the narrator; he does not even tell us Gene's last name until the sixth chapter, and then only incidentally. The name of the narrator is unimportant, inasmuch as we are listening to the author, Knowles himself. The book is narrated from the point of view of a student returning to Devon fifteen years after graduation. The narrator allows himself to be transported into the past, into a very special kind of preparatory existence for life on the outside. The narrator therefore has fifteen years' hindsight. He is able to understand more in retrospect than he originally could in anticipation. The wisdom of Gene Forrester is the wisdom of John Knowles as a matured young man. The narrator Gene Forrester realizes that he fought the real war while still at Devon. Since graduating Gene has been in the army; he went to boot camp but the war ended sooner than anyone expected. As the narrator states, "I never killed anybody, and I never developed an intense level of hatred for the enemy. Because my war ended before I ever put on a uniform; I was on active duty all my time at school; I killed my enemy there." Gene understands this now, fifteen years later; it is important to remember that he is writing about something long in the past, even though the story is so vivid that it seems to be the present. Gene realizes now - but did not originally - that each of his friends was almost unconsciously trying to erect a defense against a suspected threat, the war.

THE UNIQUENESS OF FINNY

Finny is the only boy at Devon who does not actually fear the war. As a competitive sportsman, Finny feels no need to erect a barrier between himself and the war. In fact, after his accident, he fears that he will not be able to be in the war. When he does not hear from the various American armed services -Marines, Navy, etc. - he even writes to Russia and China, to see whether he can perhaps be in the war by fighting in their armies. He creates fantastic illusions to replace the reality of the war because he fears he will not be able to enlist. He alone, however, does not erect what Knowles visualizes as a private Maginot Line.

From the beginning of the novel, Knowles has made it very clear that Finny is unique, is a special kind of human being. He exerts a hypnotic and charismatic charm over Gene and the other boys. He realizes that some of his actions - like establishing the Devon Winter Olympics - were escapes from the reality of the war, a war whose actuality is brought home through the tragic destruction of Edwin Lepellier, or Leper as he was called. Leper's tragedy becomes Finny's confrontation with his own idea that the war did not really exist, that it was the fabrication of a bunch of fat, middle-aged men whose self-interests perpetuated the gigantic rumor of war.

THE SETTING

When the novel begins, it is the summer of 1942. America is at war and summer session is open at the Devon School in New Hampshire. Newsreels and magazines are presenting pictures of war to the whole country. Bombs are being dropped by America on Central Europe. The summer is a moment in history, and Knowles offers us some of the characteristics of that moment:

"The war was and is reality for me. I still instinctively live and think in its atmosphere. These are some of its characteristics: Franklin Delano Roosevelt is the President of the United States, and he always has been. The other two eternal world leaders are Winston Churchill and Josef Stalin. America is not, never has been, and never will be what the songs and poems call it, a land of plenty. Nylon, meat, gasoline, and steel are rare. There are too many jobs and not enough workers. Money is very easy to earn, but rather hard to spend, because there isn't very much to buy. Trains are always late and always crowded with 'servicemen.' The war will always be fought very far from America and it will never end."

This then is the picture of America as a nation involved in a war being fought on foreign soil. Knowles is able to recollect the atmosphere of America in that distant summer of 1942.

SIXTEEN-YEAR-OLDS

It is important to bear in mind that the boys in the story are sixteen years old. They are not quite old enough to fight for their country. They are regarded by the adult world as the last people in the youthful world. Adults want the sixteen-year-olds to enjoy themselves now while they can, because soon they will be fighting to protect these same adults. The adult world is anxious for the boys to have a last happy period in their life before they go to war. The narrator states his belief that sixteen years old is the natural age for a human being to be.

TECHNIQUE AND STYLE

The basic technique employed by Knowles is the use of youthful point of view. Because the narrator slips back into his past world, into the time when he actually was a student at Devon, the style of expression becomes that of a sixteen-year-old boy. Knowles' technique is to transport the reader back into that private world, and his sentence structure, dialogue, use of idiom, suggestion of terror, and reference to the landscape all blend together to create the exact mood and circumstances that prevailed at Devon in 1942. The dialogue is crisp and explosive; the emotions are given expression in ways we expect from sixteen-year-olds. The landscape is depicted impressionistically; that is, we learn the geography of the world at Devon through selective impressions. Devon arises between old houses nearby on Gilman Street; there is the Far Common, a wide open ground, and there is the, First Academy Building. There is the Field House for athletic equipment known as The Cage; there are the Playing Fields. There are New England Elms, three dormitories, and a grove of trees alongside a river. The world in which the narrator moves is in fact very small in a physical sense, but Knowles' technique of seeing this world through the eyes of a student transforms it into a universe. The proportions are monumental, for things seem bigger than they are.

DEVON'S UNIVERSALITY

One reason that Knowles transforms the world of Devon into a larger one is that he wants Devon to be considered typical of the world inhabited by all sixteen-year-old boys at this moment in history. Devon thus acquires a universality, becomes, in other words, representative of all boys' schools in America in the summer of 1942. Devon becomes a symbol of "separate peace" enjoyed - but also abused - by those young men who do not yet need to be off fighting a war. Devon becomes a place in the imagination, not simply a place in New Hampshire. Devon becomes a universal symbol for a certain framework of experience - the experience of separate peace - just as Eden is always a symbol for a framework of innocence.

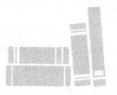

A SEPARATE PEACE

CHAPTERS 1 - 4

. . . .

Note

In order to discuss certain **themes** and the development of the different characters, it is useful to divide Knowles' *A Separate Peace* into three sections, each about four chapters of the book.

CHAPTER ONE

The narrator of the novel, Gene Forrester (we do not learn his name until later in the book) returns to the Devon School in New Hampshire from which he graduated fifteen years ago. He walks slowly through the town (it has no name) and across the Devon campus and athletic fields until he discovers a particular tree near a river. He comes in out of the rain and the narration switches back to the past; the narrator begins to speak as a student once again. There are five boys present and the leader, Phineas, dares everyone to jump from a branch of the tree out over the bank into the river. Phineas jumps, Gene jumps, but the other three - Edwin Lepellier (called Leper), Chet Douglas, and Bobby Zane - are too scared to jump. On the way back to dinner, Phineas and Gene fight for amusement and in so doing make a silent agreement that because of fighting they will be too late to eat dinner, that is, they will thereby break a rule.

Comment: Purpose Of The Chapter

The opening establishes a large number of important facts and ideas. In the first place, Gene's walk across the landscape at Devon is a piece of skillful narrative; as Gene describes his surroundings we, as readers, also become acquainted with them; what is recollection for the speaker is introduction for the reader.

Secondly, and most importantly, the seeds of the relationship between Phineas and Gene are sown. Gene, after all, is the only one of the four other boys who is willing to respond to Phineas "dare" to jump from the tree. This makes Gene special in Phineas' eyes. When Phineas begins to fight with Gene after tripping him, both boys realize they share a distrust and hatred for a regimental life. That they must hurry in order to eat dinner at the right time suddenly strikes them both as odious necessity. Having to obey the rule regarding the time for eating epitomizes having to obey all the other rules which dictate the behavior of students at a private preparatory school in New England. When Phineas trips Gene and jumps on him, he is, in fact, challenging Gene to be disobedient. It is an event which parallels jumping out of the tree. When minutes later Gene tackles Phineas, it is his way of consenting to rebellion. Just as he had been willing to be "dared" into jumping from the tree, so he is willing to "dare" to break the school rules and miss supper. In the jumping and in both fights, then, the bond between Phineas and Gene is cemented. They will have a very special relationship to each other throughout the book, and Knowles has skillfully suggested their uniqueness in the opening episodes.

Establishing The War Theme

Another of the purposes of the opening chapter is to introduce the theme of war. Knowles wants the reader to realize from the start that there is an actual war taking place at Devon. This is the subtle war among the boys themselves. To remind us that America was at war when the story takes place, the very first paragraph suggests that in 1942 the school was not as shiny as it now is because at that time there was a war on. We also learn that this summer session of school at Devon has been designed as part of the national war effort; classes must keep going all the time because students may be sent off to war any minute. The tree from which Phineas and Gene jump has been mastered by older boys; but Gene and his friends are all in the class known as Upper Middler and no Upper Middler had ever jumped from the tree. The point is that Phineas and his group are all young and not of draft age. Boys who had jumped out of the tree before are now all off fighting.

SYMBOLISM OF THE TREE

When Phineas leaps out of the tree down into the water, he cries out, "Here's my contribution to the war effort!" For Phineas, jumping out of the tree is an act of war; symbolically, the tree is a troopship which is being torpedoed. It is necessary for the imaginary soldiers to abandon the ship when it is being torpedoed and thus Phineas jumps overboard into the water.

As a soldier, Phineas feels that it is very important to perform manly acts of valor. Jumping out of the tree is a courageous act; it is dangerous to jump but nevertheless necessary. In war one must be willing to make sacrifices and to forget fear. In order to prove to Phineas that he too is courageous, Gene feels he must jump. It is the only action which a good soldier can take if he wants the respect of his men. This is why Gene is accepted as Phineas' special friend; Gene wins Phineas' respect as a fellow soldier when he jumps from the tree.

FEAR

It is logical to assume that where there is courage, there is also fear. Gene hints that he is frightened from the very beginning of his recollection. He recalls the "well known fear which had surrounded and filled" the whole school when he had been a student there; he feels "fear's echo." When he climbs up into the tree, he is filled with "a sensation of alarm all the way to [his] tingling fingers." In short, Gene is filled with various indefinable fears - he is afraid of the physical act of jumping from the tree on the one hand, and of Phineas' power to induce him to jump on the other. He is, above all, afraid to reject Phineas' dare. That the other three boys are afraid to jump is of course evident from the fact that they do not jump. This opening symbolic act of courage suggests the atmosphere of the entire book, which is filled with confrontations of frightening actions.

OVER-ALL SIGNIFICANCE

By establishing the **theme** of war, by introducing the tree as a symbol, and by depicting the fear the boys have of jumping from the tree, Knowles creates a vivid world filled with potentially frightening challenges. Phineas has coldly executed a war maneuver, but the others are not able to do so because of their very human fear. And even though Gene jumps, he realizes that he is still very much afraid of jumping. The adolescent world is attracted to that which is terrifying.

Knowles feels that for many boys, actually going off to fight in a real war is not half so frightening as fighting the war which exists in preparatory school. It is easier for a mature man to face a foreign enemy than it is for a young boy to prove himself to his peers. To prove oneself one must perform acts of heroism, acts which can be interpreted as brave or courageous. Such an act is leaping out of the tree. It is harder to perform this act than it is to jump from an actual ship which has been torpedoed. Thus the first chapter establishes the central **theme** of the book, that the war which must be won by every young man is the war against the challenges to human fear, challenges which are particularly explicit and terrifying in the adolescent world represented by Devon in the summer of 1942.

CHAPTER TWO

Mr. Prud'homme, a master, stops by the boys' room to scold them for missing dinner again - the ninth meal they have skipped in only two weeks. Phineas explains that their jumping out of the tree caused them to be late, but they felt that jumping was something they had to do as a kind of toughening up for the war. After all, Phineas argues, they will be seventeen by the end of the summer and the draft age may well be lowered to seventeen by that time. Mr. Prud'homme accepts the explanation because he, like the other adults at Devon, feels sorry for the boys who will soon have to go to war.

Phineas decides to wear a pink shirt as an "emblem" of his happiness over the recent American bombings of Central Europe. In the afternoon the boys go to the traditional tea given by Mr. Patch-Withers, the acting headmaster of the summer session. Phineas wears the Devon School tie around his waist as a belt. When Mr. Patch-Withers is shocked, Phineas explains that the tie, like the pink shirt, is a symbol of America's bombing of Central Europe. Once again Phineas' skill as a debater emerges as Mr. Patch-Withers is lenient about Phineas' violation of a rule. Thus on two occasions in the chapter Phineas "gets away" with breaking a rule.

In the end of the chapter, Phineas and Gene jump from the tree together, as the first act in the formation of what they decide to call The Super Suicide Society of the Summer Session. Gene almost falls off the branch but Phineas prevents the fall and they make a safe jump.

Comment: Breaking The Rules

It is very significant that Phineas deliberately breaks school rules. In the first incident, missing dinner, Phineas is forgiven by Mr. Prud'homme and thus Knowles is able to demonstrate the special privileges sixteen-year-olds enjoyed in the summer of 1942. At this particular moment in history, it is all right to break the rules. The boys' youthful fun and playful rebellion is, to the masters, a reminder of what peace is like. The masters are willing to be lenient because on the one hand they are heartened by the boys' "peace" and on the other hand because they realize the boys will soon be off at war. Thus it is not at all surprising that Mr. Patch-Withers also fails to become enraged at Phineas' flagrant and irresponsible misuse of the Devon tie.

Breaking the rules, further, also shows Phineas' unique power. Knowles slowly and meticulously allows us to see more of Phineas' strength as the story progresses. Gene is amazed when Mr. Prud'homme does not punish Phineas. He is certain that Mr. Patch-Withers will punish Phineas; when Phineas "gets away" with breaking the rules a second time, Gene realizes that Phineas has a private, particular, hypnotic charm over people. Phineas has the ability to make the masters sympathize with him. His sincere and outspoken support of American victory in the war outside can hardly be questioned. The masters realize that to punish Phineas is, in effect, to condemn supporting American troops. For Phineas is determined to be part of the American force, even if that part will be acted out on the playing fields of Devon.

THE WAR ON THE OUTSIDE

Knowles is careful to make Phineas' pink shirt emblematic of the recent American air attacks on Central Europe. Knowles wants us to realize that the boys at Devon had a fairly clear knowledge of the way the war on the outside was shaping up. The newspapers and the weekly newsreels are filled with the pictures of the bombings. But this is all the boys can know. That is, although they see pictures of the real war, they cannot really understand what it is like. Phineas wants desperately to be a part of that real war. As he explains to Mr. Patch-Withers, "when you come right down to it the school is involved in everything that happens in the war, it's all the same war and the same world, and I think Devon ought to be included." The fact is, however, that Devon is not a part of the real war. By definition, that would be impossible. The inhabitants of the school have no choice but to enjoy the luxury of "a separate peace," but Knowles wants us to realize that to the boys at Devon the war on the outside is the focus of curiosity; they know it exists but they do not understand it.

THE SUPER SUICIDE SOCIETY

It is Phineas' idea to create a formal club whose membership will be limited only to those who are brave. As the only available test of bravery is jumping from the tree, Phineas and Gene will automatically be the first members of what will rapidly become a very elite club. Any boy who is brave enough to "leap" will create a partnership with the other brave boys. Phineas wants desperately to enlarge the significance of jumping from the tree. This is seen particularly as he gropes toward a name for the club. First there is the mere suggestion of a suicide society; next it becomes The Suicide Society of the Summer Session; finally, it is The Super Suicide Society of the Summer Session. That is, this new club will represent only the extremely courageous boys and Phineas, who was the first to jump, is naturally the most courageous boy.

It is difficult to be certain as to why Knowles chose to call the club a "suicide" one. Phineas interprets jumping from the tree as symbolic of strength and of a willingness to die. But this willingness is not the same thing as actual death itself. The implication is that Phineas is asking the boys to give their lives for the cause. They should not only symbolically be ready to die; they should in fact die. This is, after all, a bizarre preparation for dying in the real war on the outside. Phineas is choosing to call the jumping an even greater symbolic act - that of suicide.

Foreshadowing The Accident

At the very end of the chapter, Gene stumbles and almost falls off. Phineas' hand darts out suddenly and saves Gene from toppling off the branch to the ground below. Gene notes that he might have fallen on the bank and broken his back, had it not been for Phineas. This near-accident foreshadows the fall which will come later on. At that time, Phineas will fall to the ground and Gene will be unable to help him; in fact, it will be suggested that Gene even wanted Phineas to fall. Thus now, in Chapter Two, this closing **episode** foreshadows the tragedy which will come later on. Knowles is forcing us to contemplate the reality of the horror and pain which could result if one of the boys were actually to fall from the tree. In other words, though jumping is symbolic of great danger, it is at the same time something which is in reality dangerous in itself. Gene realizes this as he almost falls, and his understanding later on of the horror of Phineas' fall is strengthened by this brief flirtation with disaster.

STYLE

The student should begin to understand the simplicity of Knowles' **diction**. The narration is offered in easily comprehended terms; there are no obscure **allusions** or unfamiliar words. The vocabulary is basically simple. The dialogue consists primarily of brief exchanges. There are occasional long answers, as for example when Phineas explains himself to Mr. Prud'homme or Mr. Patch-Withers. But among the boys themselves the exchanges are short and rapid. It is as if Knowles wants to point up the disparity between the boys' simplicity of speech and their complexity of thought. That is, the boys talk as if some things - the war, jumping from the tree, etc. - are basically uncomplicated, when in fact they know that these things are very complicated.

Phineas tends to ask questions which can be answered yes or no, or at least in no more than a few words.

The brevity of the dialogue between Gene and Phineas also suggests the atmosphere of being at war. When a war is on, one simply does not have time for long speeches and directions. Phineas therefore speaks more or less like a field lieutenant issuing orders to his men; he is presiding over an imaginary squadron and speaks quickly and to the point; the suggestion is that every minute counts when one is at war and therefore not too many words can be expended.

The tone of the novel is consistently one of reminiscence saturated with fear; along with remembrance comes the newly reactivated set of fears. There is little nostalgia and much anxiety. The tone - that is, the writer's attitude toward his material - is matter-of-fact but not at all romanticized; the reality of the past stays a reality. The defects of that past are not glossed over.

CHAPTER THREE

As the chapter opens we learn that many boys at Devon have become interested in joining The Super Suicide Society of the Summer Session. To accommodate all of the members who must be initiated, the club meets every night now. Phineas and Gene are charter members and they must open the meeting each night by jumping out of the tree; the other boys are "trainees." We hear of Phineas' love of rules - his own, not Devon's - and then we find the creation of a new kind of war game called blitzball in which everyone is everyone else's enemy. Phineas has almost unconsciously designed a game which will allow him to excel. His tendency to excel is further brought out as he decides to break an old school swimming record; he does so but only

Gene observes him and he is sworn to secrecy because Phineas does not want anyone to know that he has set a new record. Real swimming is in the ocean, Phineas asserts, and thus the two boys bicycle to the beach. After swimming, eating supper at a hot-dog stand, and having a beer at a bar, the two boys find a comfortable spot on the beach and settle down to spend the night there. Just before falling to sleep, Phineas confides to Gene that he considers him his "best pal." Gene thinks he feels the same way about Phineas but he is not sure.

Comment: Establishing New Rules

Whereas in Chapter Two we found Phineas concerned with breaking the established "rules" of life at Devon, we now find him concerned with establishing new "rules" of his own. Gene notices for the first time that Finny (another of Phineas' names) lives by a certain set of private rules; two, for example, are that one should tell the literal truth, and one should say one's prayers at night "because it might turn out that there is a God." Another of Finny's rules is that one must always win at sports. For Finny a rule is a way of life, a necessity, and, inevitably, a challenge that must be met. Attempts are not sufficient; only victory is allowed under Finny's rules.

One of the boys, Bobby Zane, suggests a game to be called "blitzkrieg ball"; Finny modifies it to be simply blitz-ball. It is important to understand that a blitzkrieg (German: "lightning war") was a term coined to describe the rapidity of modern war and was a popular word in the news coverage of the war in Europe. The boys' game, in other words, is a new kind of war. Phineas decides all of the rules of the new game. Finny speaks of these rules as if they should be obvious to everyone - even though the game has just been invented. Finny, in other words, has a certain instinct for rules and consequently feels they are very important.

THE IMPORTANCE OF BLITZBALL

While the game of blitzball allows us to see Finny's overpowering convictions about creating rules, it also allows Knowles to introduce once again the **theme** of the war taking place at Devon. Finny wants the game to represent war. Thus there are to be no teams; instead, everyone is an enemy. Everyone is at war with everyone else; as Finny says, "since we're all enemies, we can and will turn on each other all the time." To reproduce the conditions of real war, Phineas knows that it is important that everyone be kept in continuous danger. Having teams would provide a certain kind of security and in war there is no security at all. Phineas seems to forget that real armies have comrades fighting together, because for him every man is the enemy. This is brought out later in the book when Phineas, anxious to fight but unable to be in the American army, thinks about fighting in one of the other armies such as that of China.

The way blitzball is played is quite simple: one person carries a large ball while others try to knock him down by throwing themselves against the runner. Gene realizes that Phineas has invented a game which he can play every well, being naturally athletic and a strong runner. In any case, blitzball is extremely popular - as was jumping from the tree - and the conclusion is that Phineas has successfully introduced a second kind of war game. Only it is not simply a game; rather, it is brutal suggestion of what real war on the outside is like.

THE WAR ON THE OUTSIDE

In Chapter Two Knowles reminded us of the boys' awareness of the real war on the outside by reference to the Allied bombing of Central Europe. Now, in Chapter Three, we again are told of Gene's feelings and awareness regarding that real war. We hear of the various world leaders - President Roosevelt, Winston Churchill, and Stalin - and we hear of what the general image of America was during the war years. During this period all of the newspapers are filled with strange maps of distant battlefields; people listen to newscasts many times every day; there is little luxury and recreation available; the entire country seems colored olive drab as uniformed men crowd into various bus and railroad depots. In short, almost everywhere in America there is evidence that the country is at war. Everywhere, that is, except Devon. The seniors are busy doing calisthenics, running through the woods, "off somewhere, shaping up for the war." But for the Upper Middlers like Gene and Phineas, the war was simply not yet exerting any real pressure. Thus, synthetic war had to be created and blitzball is one result.

BREAKING THE SWIMMING RECORD

When Phineas sees a bronze plaque at the school pool on which there is engraved a record of the 100 Yards Free Style - set by A. Hopkins Parker, 1940, in 53.0 seconds - he feels certain that he can break that record. This is a major facet of Finny's personality: the rule is to win. In effect, A. Hopkins Parker's record becomes a new enemy and Finny must vanquish it. With Gene timing his performance with a stop watch, Finny swims and betters the time by .7 second. When Gene worries about whether it will "count," it being an unofficial time, Finny replies, "well of course it won't count." It is not important to Finny that he broke the record and can thus have his name placed on a plaque. What is important is that he has won; in besting A. Hopkins Parker he has played according to his self-made rule which says "win in sports," and, at the same time, has vanquished another fictitious enemy.

FINNY'S HONESTY

At the end of Chapter Three Finny admits to Gene that he is his best friend; as he explains to Gene: "you can't come to the shore with just anybody and you can't come by yourself, and at this teen-age period in life the proper person is your best pal, which is what you are." It would not occur to Finny to hold back this emotion; Gene is amazed because at Devon one simply does not state one's feelings so openly. The importance of Finny's admission is that we understand at last the extreme honesty at the center of his being. Like winning at sports, being honest is a rule which Finny has made. There is no point, he notes early in the book, in saying that you are a little taller than you really are; similarly, there is no point in not saying a whole truth. He has no reason to say he likes Gene, or considers him one of his good friends, when the plain truth is that he is sure that Gene is his "best pal."

GENE'S DOUBTS

Gene wants to say that Finny is his best pal but is unable to do so. From the very beginning of the book, Gene has made it clear that he is not certain he likes Finny. Gene has seen Finny's hypnotic power over the other boys, and even over the masters. Gene therefore is slightly afraid of Finny and this prevents him from giving him unqualified approval. It is very important to realize that these doubts about Finny exist from the very start, because they make Gene's guilt later on very logical. Because he has had doubts about his own feelings towards Finny all along, it is hard to ignore them later on after the accident.

CHAPTER FOUR

Gene wakes up on the beach the next morning. Shortly, Finny wakes up and goes swimming; it is 6:30 and Gene has a trigonometry examination at Devon, a three-hour bicycle ride away. They return just in time and Gene fails the examination - for the first time in his life. Finny tells Gene that he works too hard and Gene suspects, suddenly, that Finny is jealous of Gene's academic achievements. Gene realizes that if he were to be considered the best student at Devon, that is by winning the Scholastic Achievement Citation and being chosen to deliver the commencement speech, then he would be even with Finny. Gene would be the best student and Finny would be the best athlete. Gene knows that Finny must be best and that he cannot be best if Gene becomes even with him through his studies. We see the effects of wartime psychology as Gene carefully decides that he and Finny are locked in complete enmity rather than friendship.

Finny announces Leper's intention of leaping from the tree tonight and coaxes Gene away from his studies. But first, Finny expresses surprise that Gene needs to study at all - and Gene, consequently, is no longer certain whether or not Finny is jealous. That night Gene and Finny are standing together on the limb, preparing for the jump, when Gene feels his knee bend, the branch shake, and then sickeningly, sees Finny crash to the hard ground beneath. In a state of shock, Gene walks out to the end of the limb and leaps successfully into the river.

Comment: Collapse Of School Rules

We have seen earlier the continuous weakening of school rules and now, in Chapter Four, we realize that all school rules have been forgotten. As the war on the outside has entered into the masters' psychology with increasing gravity, they have ignored the maintenance of discipline over the boys. This is brought out when Phineas and Gene explain to Mr. Prud'homme that they spent the night sleeping on the beach. Mr. Prud'homme reacts with interest but completely fails to realize that the boys, in sleeping on the beach, have violated a school rule. The implication is that at Devon School rules and discipline have completely collapsed.

AMBIGUOUS RIVALRY

During the course of the chapter we see Gene's ambiguous feelings about Finny. On the one hand Gene suspects that Finny is jealous, that Finny detests him for being a better student. On the other hand, Gene sees a certain curious nonchalance in Finny regarding all academic matters in general and Gene's accomplishments in particular. When Finny understands, for the first time, that it is necessary for Gene to study, he advises him to skip the meeting that night of The Super Suicide Society and study instead. Finny claims that it simply has never occurred to him that Gene, being so smart, needs to study.

Part of Gene's doubts about Finny's friendship and the quality of the general relationship between the two boys is due to his awareness of Finny's unusually highly motivated desire to excel. We recall that Finny designed blitzball in a way which would allow him to be the best player. There is also the subtle mathematics which Gene uses: if he is the best student and also pretty good at athletics, while Finny is the best athlete and a pretty bad student, then Gene is not only even to Finny; he is better than Finny.

WARTIME PSYCHOLOGY

Part of Gene's reason for suspecting Finny is simply the fact of war and the psychology which exists in those participating in war. We first see the competitive aspects of war as Gene summarizes the suspected enmity between himself and Finny. We see the almost insane way in which Gene talks to himself. His comments suggest a diseased outlook, an attitude toward life and friends suddenly marred by the reality of wartime conditions. We should recall Finny's argument that there can be no friendships and alliances in war. In blitzball it is every man for himself. Why shouldn't it be that way in all aspects of life at Devon? Thus Gene begins to believe: "We were even after all, even in enmity. The deadly rivalry was on both sides after all." The wartime psychology, the effects of leaping from the tree and of blitzball, and the general atmosphere at Devon all converge to shatter emotions of trust and sincerity. It is easy under these circumstances for Gene to convince himself that Finny is his enemy, that Finny has consciously sought to undermine Gene's opportunities to excel in his studies. This is the psychology of war, and this is evidence that the war has invaded and pervaded life at Devon.

THE VOCABULARY OF WAR

Knowles is very careful to describe events and emotions at Devon with words which are usually used to describe war. Reading through Chapter Four we see many war terms - enmity, deadly rivalry, coldly driving ahead, treachery, on guard, new attacks, redoubling my effort, and cold trickery. These and similar words and expressions borrowed from the vocabulary of war are carefully employed to saturate the atmosphere of the story with the idea of war. This idea is continually suggested by both oblique and direct references to various aspects of waging a war, the attacking and retreating, the fortifying and the recuperating, etc. Knowles never allows much time to elapse without some suggestion of the idea of war, for war is an overpowering, omnipresent phenomenon and cannot easily or realistically be minimized or forgotten. The world at Devon is filled with war, with doubts, with mistrust, and with undefined and misunderstood feelings of enmity and rivalry; to maintain this world Knowles relies on the vocabulary of war.

THE FALL OF PHINEAS

Finny's fall from the tree is the main event of the novel. It marks the conclusion of the first major portion of the book, for after Finny's fall nothing can be the same. We must understand the fall in reference to Gene's doubts, which have been increasingly vivid during the chapter. Because Finny's fall arrives shortly after Gene's expression of the enmity between himself and Finny, it is very logical for Gene to feel guilty about Finny's fall. As Gene has come to distrust Finny, perhaps he has now purposely caused Finny to fall. Granted that this intention was unconscious, it nevertheless may have existed. Knowles intentionally describes the fall in a very rapid fashion. Gene does not really know precisely what happened in that brief moment when he felt his knees bend and the limb quiver. Perhaps he was jouncing Finny off the limb; perhaps he himself momentarily was losing his balance. There is no way for him to know and because of his feelings about Finny presented earlier in the chapter, he realizes he may be guilty.

Finny's fall is both literal and metaphorical. That is, when Finny falls from the tree, he also "falls" from his position of superior athlete at Devon. No longer is Finny to reign supreme in sports and, when we recall his rule - "win in sports" - we realize that for Finny the fall must be a tragedy. Falling from the tree is, further, symbolic of the loss of Finny's power to control and manipulate the other boys. There is a poetic justice in the fact that Finny is finally harmed by his own wartime invention. It was his idea to form a suicide society whose members would jump often from the tree. It was his idea that the boys at Devon should be willing to risk their lives when the country is at war. And Finny's fall, after all, is the loss of his life, in as much as his life consisted of playing sports and striving to excel. With his fall, this life as a great athlete is brought to a tragic and unexpected end. His desires, his feelings of superiority, his hypnotic charm over the other boys, and his all-important example of a way of life being presented to Gene are brought down when he crashes to the hard bank beneath the tree.

IMPORTANCE OF THE CHAPTER

Chapter Four is a turning point in the novel because at last we see the brutality which is potential in the special, private war among the boys. It is not simply Finny's fall from the tree to the bank that suggests the brutality of war. Rather, it is the introduction of adult suspicion, of belligerence and misunderstanding. Real war, with its absence of trust and its enmities, makes human communication very difficult or impossible. And as one's ability to know others decreases, one realizes that it is also harder to know oneself. This is the "message" of the chapter: in war, one cannot have self-knowledge. Finny's fall is a horrible fact of war. It is the stark reality of pain introduced into an atmosphere of unreal trouble. The illusion has become reality; jumping from the tree is not simply symbolic of risking one's life. Now jumping from the tree means real danger. Finny's tragedy provides a new example to the boys at Devon and, simultaneously, introduces Gene to the problem of personal identity and self-knowledge.

A SEPARATE PEACE

CHAPTERS 5 - 7

. . . .

CHAPTER FIVE

When the chapter begins, Finny is in the school infirmary with a "shattered" leg. Gene bears the private burden of guilt. For some curious reason, he puts on Finny's shoes, pants, and even his shirt; that is, momentarily he imagines that he is Finny and the sensation excites him. Dr. Stanpole, the acting school physician, informs Gene that Finny wants to see him. Together in the infirmary room, Gene and Finny discuss the "accident" together; Finny recalls having reached out to grab Gene's hand before falling. Finny also recollects a strange feeling and the implication is that Finny had a momentary feeling that Gene wanted him to fall. Gene is about to confess his responsibility for Finny's fall when Dr. Stanpole interrupts their discussion.

Finny is taken in an ambulance to his home near Boston and Gene returns to his hometown somewhere in the South. In September, en route to Devon in New Hampshire, Gene stops at

Finny's home. At first they exchange stories and talk about the summer; then Gene confesses that he caused Finny's accident. Finny replies that Gene is crazy and had done no such thing.

Comment: The Desire To Confess

Few people are able to bear the weight of guilt and Gene is no exception. Because of his earlier hostility (either real or imagined) toward Finny, Gene is convinced that he caused Finny's fall from the tree. It bothers Gene that none of the other boys seem suspicious of him. No one says anything to Gene which would suggest that they consider him to blame for what has happened to Finny. Thus Gene must bear the guilt alone. His desire to confess is clarified when he starts to tell Finny what he thinks must have happened. Knowles purposely has Dr. Stanhope enter the room and interrupt the confession. Gene must endure his private feelings of unworthiness for the duration of the entire summer. Then, when he is at last near Finny again he immediately goes to Finny and confesses. The longer the time waiting to confess, the greater the conviction of guilt has become. Whereas at first Gene only suspected his guilt, he later is sure of it.

FINNY'S AMBIVALENCE

Knowles makes it clear that even Phineas is not certain that Gene is not to blame. Finny carefully explains that he had tried to grab hold of Gene just before his fall and, further, that he had a peculiar feeling about the cause of the accident. When he tells Gene he is sorry about having had that feeling, the implication is that the feeling was one of fear that Gene wanted to hurt him. When Finny so vigorously refuses to accept Gene's confession, he is trying to convince himself that his best friend really is his best friend. In other words, Finny must believe in Gene's sincere friendship but at the same time must reconcile his suspicions that Gene could have intended the accident to happen. Once the accident has taken place, Finny has a new and deep ambivalence toward Gene, for just as Gene doubts himself, so must Finny doubt Gene. But Finny, even more than Gene, wants to believe the best about Gene. Nevertheless, Finny does have ambivalent feelings even at this early date following his fall and Knowles introduces them now so that later there will be a greater logic to the trial when Finny is forced to recall the accident as best he can.

IMPORTANCE OF PLOT

The events of Knowles' book fall into a harmonious pattern. Aspects of character are introduced early in the book and then are suggested a second time later on. The plot of the book is constructed in such a way as to make actions and their significance return upon themselves. There is the plain logic, of course, of having Finny return to a home which is not too far from Boston. After all, Boston is a natural stopping place on Gene's return trip to Devon. Thus it is "convenient" that he is able to stop off and see Finny with such ease. When the tree is first chosen as a place for adventure and daring, we are hardly aware of the extent of that adventure. Only later, after we have returned to the tree several times, do we realize the wisdom of Knowles' choice. To fall from a tree is, again, a very "convenient" way of symbolizing "falling" from high to low estate. The built-in **metaphor** has been planned with the entire plot in mind. And this is characteristic of the book: at every point of the story, Knowles knows precisely where he is heading. He seems to have the last page in mind when he writes the first page. The plot is designed with precision and functions in an economical way. Nothing is introduced that will not connect logically with everything else; the strong symbolic and logical ties between blitzball and jumping from the tree are representative of all the bonds in the entire plot.

THE PERVASIVE ACCIDENT

After Finny's fall from the tree, the mood of the book changes slightly; along with the idea of war, we now have the idea of injury. Finny's accident becomes a pervasive subject. It occupies almost the entirety of Gene's thinking. It naturally changes the life of Finny himself. All the boys are always aware of the tragedy that has befallen Finny. The atmosphere of the book, the world of Devon, and the minds of the boys are all filled with the idea of Finny's fall. The masters at Devon feel sorry for Finny. But even more importantly, they feel sorry that such a tragedy could have come to a sixteen-year-old boy. We recall that early in the novel it was suggested that there was something special about the sixteen-year-olds: they were exempt from the tragedies of war. But with Phineas' accident their world is no longer private. The masters, the students, and (less obviously) Phineas himself all feel sorry for Phineas. His accident is an influence on them and on their philosophical detachment from the reality of war.

GENE'S ASSUMPTION OF FINNY'S IDENTITY

It is important to remember the **episode** in which Gene puts on Finny's clothes; there is the deliberate suggestion of a motive for Gene's having made Finny fall. For when Gene pretends to be Finny, it is the first time he has ever been able to do so. That is, only with Finny "out of the way" is Gene able to form an equation between himself and Finny. We recall that earlier Gene had spent considerable time attempting to decide whether he and Finny were in fact "even." Now, when dressed in Finny's clothes before the mirror, Gene exclaims, "I was Phineas, Phineas to the life." This, in other words, is the first time that Gene has actually been able to become Phineas. The importance of this is that Gene's exhilaration over becoming Phineas suggests to him that he might consciously have caused Phineas' accident. The "sense of transformation" which Gene experiences, then, connects positively with the guilt which Gene has harbored since the accident. Having enjoyed this transformation the night before, Gene's first trip to Phineas in the infirmary is automatically filled with guilt and despair, pivotal emotions of the new world established by Finny's fall.

CHAPTER SIX

It is the 163rd fall at the Devon School (there had been only one summer session in the school's history) and at the convocation in the chapel the boys are told that everything will continue at Devon as it always has. But Gene cannot help reflecting back on the "gypsy days" of the summer and the change that they have initiated. We hear for the first time of Brinker Hadley, a class official and politician, who lives across the hall from Gene. Gene reports to crew practice down at the Naguamset tidewater river where he meets the crew manager Cliff Quackenbush. Gene begins his duties as assistant crew manager, although he has never managed sports before.

Quackenbush refers meanly to Gene as being "maimed" and Gene attacks him as a reply. For Gene it is a war campaign being fought in defense of Phineas who of course really is "maimed." Shortly later, Mr. Ludsbury, a returning Devon hall master, questions Gene about "gaming" and other infractions of the school rules which occurred during the summer session, and concludes by scolding Gene and the others for having taken advantage of Mr. Prud'homme. Finny phones Gene and, after ascertaining that they would be roommates when he returned, becomes angry at Gene for being a crew manager rather than actually playing at sports. Finny explains that because he himself is no longer able to play sports, Gene must play for him; Gene realizes that perhaps this is what he was meant to be from the very beginning, a part of Finny.

Comment: The Atmosphere At Devon

The opening of the fall session is very different from the atmosphere of the summer session. As Knowles points out, the summer session was an exception, an isolated example of a way of life at Devon. That is all ended now and there is to be a return to normalcy (to borrow President Harding's phrase). There is of course the recognizable disparity between the "continuity" which is being discussed and the lack of it which is visible. Five of Devon's younger teachers, for example, are absent at convocation because they are off at war. One of the teachers, moreover, arrives at convocation in his old naval ensign's uniform. Thus the boys realize that in spite of what the masters are saying, there must be a difference between life at Devon during peacetime and life at Devon during wartime. The atmosphere of the school is thus woven out of the difference between unverbalized facts about war and recognizable evidence of war. At the same time, however, as seen in Mr. Ludsbury's remarks to Gene, there is in the Devon atmosphere the continuing sense of necessary rules.

BREAKING THE RULES AND FINNY'S ACCIDENT

Gene realizes that the much-talked-of "continuity" is nonexistent. Life at Devon can simply never be the same since the relaxation of rules during the summer session. Rules have been broken; we are reminded of this by both Gene and Mr. Ludsbury. Still, the summer session is over and there will be more compliance with rules now than before. Gene imagines that Devon had been vindicated through Finny's accident. During the summer when the boys were busily and pointedly breaking the rules, they were automatically inviting a large-scale punishment - which was rendered in the form of Finny's accident. That is, there is a fatalistic implication about Finny's fall. It is not simply a case of wondering who is responsible for the fall, but rather of wondering whether the fall was inevitable. The boys had invited their own doom by breaking the rules; as Gene asserts, "if you broke the rules, then they broke you." And we should not miss the implicit **metaphor** in the word "broke," for Phineas, after all, does have a "broken leg." He provided the "idiosyncratic, leaderless band" of boys with at least a little leadership; the boys were given direction in breaking the rules by "the eccentric notions of Phineas." And as Phineas led the breaking of the rules, so he was the one to be broken in return.

IMPORTANCE OF THE FIGHT

The fight between the veteran crew manager Cliff Quackenbush and the novice assistant crew manager Gene is basically a symbolic contest. Quackenbush is of course a despicable and unpopular person, and thus Gene is inclined to dislike him from the start. But the real reason for the fight between the two boys is of central importance. Quackenbush only figuratively refers to Gene as "maimed"; it is a typical meaningless insult for him to make. He has no idea that Gene has further, private associations with the word "maimed" through his thoughts about Phineas. The accident "maimed" Phineas for life, shattered his leg, and made it impossible for Phineas to participate in sports. Gene is extremely "touchy" about Finny's new maimed existence, and thus Quackenbush's meaningless insult explodes violently in Gene's mind and causes him to strike out at Quackenbush with the admonition to be careful about what he might say about maimed people.

Gene hits Quackenbush without knowing why he is doing so. In reflection, however, he realizes he was fighting for Finny. The struggle with Quackenbush was a small campaign, an act of war, done primarily out of loyalty to Finny. Gene has become, in one sense, an extension of Finny; he is to be courageous in Finny's behalf. Through the fight with Quackenbush he realizes his new relationship to Finny and the fact that he is still at war; the fight is the "first skirmish of a long campaign." The war emotions established in the games of the summer session are still at the center of Gene's being.

GENE'S DECISION TO MANAGE

Gene has decided to become the assistant crew manager because he does not consider it fair for him to enjoy playing sports now that Phineas is not able to do so. For Gene, it is a kind of self-denial designed by him to parallel the denial of sports to Finny. Gene's self-denial is a kind of punishment. He may feel guilty about the possibility of having caused Finny's accident, but he would feel even more guilty were he to enjoy playing sports now that sports are denied to Finny, particularly in light of their earlier rivalry in sports and the competitive aspect of their relationship as friends. What Gene does not realize at first, however, is that Phineas would not approve of his decision to manage. Only on the phone with Finny later does he realize that Finny prefers him to continue in sports for both of them; Finny is far too practical to want Gene to quit sports and prefers to have Gene representing both of them. Thus he is outraged and nonplused when Gene tells him on the phone of his decision to be assistant crew manager. And then Gene realizes that he must now be an extension of Finny; this, rather than self-denial, is to be his punishment for causing the fall from the tree.

THE IDEA OF WAR

Although it is now the 163rd fall session at the Devon School, and although the boys are theoretically pursuing a peaceful and disciplined life, the suggestion of war is still expectedly present. Aside from the visible evidence that the country is at war - such as the missing young teachers in the chapel convocation scene - there is the constant implied reference back to the "war games" of the one and only summer session. In addition to Gene's feelings of guilt about participating in sports is his strong inclination to interpret all sports as facets of war. Gene continues to perceive the war's effects in everything around him. Just as Finny's summer inventions like jumping out of the tree and blitzball had enlarged the idea of war in the boy's minds, so regular, ordinary sports sustain that idea of war. There is no real way of escaping from the evidence of the warring aspects of human existence. It is implied here, furthermore, that this aspect of existence does in fact possess a reality; it is not simply a question of Gene's imagination, for people are, at heart, inclined to war.

CHAPTER SEVEN

Brinker Hadley stops in to see Gene and congratulates him for having been able to secure a whole room for himself. Then he suggests that Gene accompany him to the Butt Room, a dungeonlike chamber in the dormitory basement where the boys are permitted to smoke. When they arrive at the Butt Room, Brinker pushes Gene into the smoke-filled room, half-jokingly saying, "Here's your prisoner." Brinker continues to tease Gene, suggesting that Gene has done away with his roommate. At first Gene is very defensive and reacts harshly to the jokes of Brinker, but slowly he begins to joke himself and the subject of Finny's accident vanishes. Brinker composes a poem pointing to the fact that the war is boring, while life at Devon continues in peace.

Heavy snow has paralyzed the railroad yards of a town south of Boston and many of the Devon boys volunteer to help shovel out the train tracks. Gene, Brinker, and others join in, but Leper goes off by himself to take photographs of beaver dams. Later, when the track has been cleared, Brinker taunts Leper for being a "naturalist" and then suddenly announces that he is going to enlist. The boys have seen the soldiers on the troop trains and Brinker feels - as they all do - that these soldiers are about the same age as they are. After Brinker's announcement, Gene also begins to think about enlisting and about the war in general, but his thoughts are interrupted when he returns to his room and finds Phineas there waiting for him.

Comment: Brinker's Accusation Of Gene

Brinker Hadley goes out of his way to make Gene uncomfortable. Brinker's first suggestion that Gene has eliminated Finny on purpose arrives in the form of congratulating Gene for having a room to himself, an unusual occurrence at Devon and one, which, by implication, could not have come about if Gene had not eliminated Finny. When Brinker shoves Gene into the Butt Room the cruel accusation is beginning to come to the surface. Brinker has just echoed Gene's own statement - "the truth will out" - in a menacing way, as if to suggest that the truth about the accident, Gene's responsibility, will be known soon enough. When Brinker then almost immediately announces, "Here's your prisoner, gentlemen, I'm turning him over to the proper authorities," Gene cannot but feel that he is being formally arraigned. What Gene is slow to understand is that Brinker may only be kidding. Later in the novel, Gene actually will have a "trial" for his part in the fall of Phineas, but at this time the trial is only playful. Were it not for the guilt which has been building in Gene already, Brinker's words would be meaningless. But as with the episode involving the fight with Quackenbush, Gene's emotions color other boys' remarks. Brinker is, of course, a cruel boy, one who would like to see some further evidence of the war. Brinker is a big shot, a big man on the campus, and when he points his finger at Gene, the latter is understandably terrified. Brinker suggests menacingly that Gene has done away with his roommate Finny. The description of "the scene of the crime... that funereal tree" illustrates that Brinker is able to imagine without difficulty the way in which Gene might have purposely pushed Finny from the tree, and his accusation of Gene is only half joking. That is, we cannot really tell whether or not Brinker is serious. The other boys present are quite obviously only playing, but we cannot tell just what Brinker feels. We see in his tormenting of Leper a capacity for cruelty, and thus he may very well honestly think Gene is guilty and may therefore be determined to prosecute him.

All in all, then, Brinker's accusation that Gene pushed Finny from the tree is catalytic: it makes Gene's suspicions of his own responsibility for Finny's fall a little more believable; and it shows the extent to which Gene is still at war, for he would not have been at all defensive about Brinker's charges had he not considered them as an "attack."

IMPORTANCE OF THE ACCUSATION TO THE PLOT

Knowles is very careful to establish connecting points in his story line. This first accusation of Gene by Brinker foreshadows the major accusation which he will make more seriously later on in the story. Brinker's utterances are, in effect, experiments. By Gene's reaction to what he says now, Brinker can calculate how Gene will respond to the treatment he will be given later. Brinker is sending up a trial balloon and it works: Gene is nervous and defensive. In this first attack, in another war game (this time a war trial), Brinker is successful. The incident advances the development of Gene's guilt on the one hand, and prepares us quite subtly for subsequent action to come. In Brinker's comments we see Knowles' reminder of what has gone before (particularly the haziness of explanations for the fall of Finny) and his concurrent suggestion of what will come later. Knowles is very expert, in short, in establishing ahead of time a certain portion of the logic behind events.

THE HUMAN TENDENCY TO CREATE EVIL

In Chapter Seven there is an important philosophical statement which has implications for the entire novel: people discover evil, and when they cannot do so, they even create evil. Knowles is suggesting that human beings need war inasmuch as they have always needed evil. Part of the attraction of things is their hidden evil. The boys play war games in the summer at Devon because they need some evil in their lives. Brinker is cruel to Gene and to Leper because he needs to be cruel sometimes and it affects Gene as well. We recall that Gene began to be suspicious of Phineas for no real reason; he had a need to discover something threatening, just as Phineas himself had a need to play dangerous games, and as Brinker has a need to torment other boys. War, Knowles feels, is basically something produced by these unfortunate needs in human beings; there will always be war because people will always need danger and will, in searching for that danger, even go so far as to create their own evil.

A SEPARATE PEACE

· ·

CHAPTER EIGHT

The chapter begins with Gene explaining to the returned Finny (now on crutches) that there are no maids because of the war. Certain Devon luxuries have had to be sacrificed. Finny does not accept Gene's views seriously, for Finny has a private vision of peace. Gene realizes that Finny needs him a great deal, particularly as Finny begins to coach Gene in preparation for the 1944 Olympics. Gene had told Finny that he was not going out for sports because "sports don't seem so important with the war on." Finny's reply is, "Have you swallowed all that war stuff?" Finny is convinced that there really is no war at all. As far as he is concerned, the whole idea of a war has been fabricated by a bunch of fat old men who, fearful or losing their jobs to younger men, want to keep the younger men going off to war. Finny explains that he knows this, while the others do not, because only he has "suffered."

Gene submits to Finny's desire that he prepare for the Olympics and tries therefore to forget about war, although the Devon faculty now uses the war to make the boys work harder. Gene runs four times around an oval walk and Mr. Ludsbury, having heard Finny's explanation that Gene is training for the Olympics, responds that this is a fine idea, but of course everyone knows that all exercise is really part of the war effort.

Comment: Finny's Private Peace

Finny is determined not to permit the war on the outside to disrupt his happy life at Devon. Where in the summer session Finny was the leader of war games and largely instrumental in establishing a wartime psychology among the boys, he now has reversed himself and become a leading spokesman for peace. His private feelings about peace constitute the largest part of his attraction for Gene, because Gene would like to share Finny's peaceful outlook. Although the news media are carrying the story of war, Gene feels that perhaps by way of the imagination he can come to share Finny's peace. Because the boys at Devon cannot really "see" the war, Finny's peaceful ideas gain credibility, particularly in light of his theory about the war.

FINNY'S THEORY ABOUT THE WAR

As a spokesman for peace, Finny reiterates continuously his theory of the war which is that there is no war. The war has been dreamed up by fat old men who fear the young pressing up behind them. Thus when Finny returns to Devon and hears Gene's explanation of why there are no maids, he is outraged and retorts that this business of there being no maids is absurd because there is no war. As the only contact the boys have with the outside world is composed of news media, Gene has to admit that it is remotely possible that Finny is right, that the pictures and broadcasts might be faked. Gene of course is anxious to believe Finny, for everyone would like to believe that there is no war.

Finny's theory that there is no war has more than the simple explanation that he prefers peaceful existence. We must remember how much Finny liked war, how he invented The Super Suicide Society and blitzball because of the war, how he thought it terrible that the boys at Devon had no real part in the war effort, and how in general he brought out the warring instincts of each of the boys. His new theory has been designed as a defense for himself. The truth is that Finny would like very much to go to war, to be a great soldier, to win in war as he has always won in sports at Devon. But now, on crutches, Finny cannot be used in the war and his feeling is simply that if he cannot be in the war, then no one else is going to be in it either. The only way in which to prevent the other boys from participating in the war is to nullify the war. Gene cannot be a part of something which does not exist. Thus Finny's whole philosophical and quasihistorical explanation of the nonexistence of the war is erected as a large superstructure beneath which he as a maimed athlete can hide. Finny has no fear of war, but instead a jealousy that others will be able to fight while he cannot. His only fear is of being left out.

SHIFT IN FACULTY ATTITUDE TOWARD WAR

As the war becomes less and less of a reality for Finny and subsequently Gene, it becomes more and more a reality for the masters at Devon. There is a gradual shift in their attitude, as the novel unfolds, away from the view that sixteen-year-old boys are deserving of a final peace, to the attitude that these boys, and boys everywhere, must prepare for the war. Whereas in the summer session the masters were apt to relax the rules, now they are apt to tighten them. The boys are being asked to try a little harder in everything they do. Gene of course feels that the faculty members are merely using the war as an excuse to make the boys work harder - something they have always wanted the boys to do. Finny of course continues to resist the Devon rules. In this chapter, for example, he persuades Gene to skip the first class of the term with him and they go to the gym instead. Because of Finny's theory of the war it would be illogical for him to submit to the faculty plea to be more conscientious because of the war. Finny's rebellion thus has a slightly different shading now that the winter term has begun. He defies the rules in order to preserve his self-made image, and not simply for the sake of defying authority in general. Finny helps Gene in sports, while Gene helps Finny in studies, but neither does so for the reason urged by the faculty. What efforts Gene and Finny make are expended by themselves for their own reasons; they will not be forced to prepare for a war which is only an illusion. Instead they will continue their enjoyment of a separate peace; they are, after all, "out of the line of fire" and there is no reason they should pretend otherwise.

TECHNIQUE: PRESERVING BRINKER'S THREAT

When Brinker Hadley meets the returned Phineas, he acts surprised, then turns to Gene and says, "So, your little plot didn't work so well after all." That is, Brinker reminds Gene that he has not relinquished his theory that Gene pushed Finny out of the tree. When Gene at first pretends not to understand the implications of Brinker's remark, Brinker replies, "You know what I'm talking, about." Brinker is determined to persecute Gene, particularly because Gene originally acted so guilty when he was first half-jokingly accused in the Butt Room of having done away with Finny in order to have a room to himself. Brinker's initial accusations posed a threat to the nervous and unsure Gene.

Knowles' technique is to maintain an atmosphere of war between Brinker and Gene. Brinker is, in effect, a threat to Gene and Knowles reminds us of this periodically. Later, there will be a formal "trial" of Gene and Knowles wants to keep the emotions building toward that **episode**. His technique therefore is to preserve Brinker's threat, remind the reader that Gene is afraid of Brinker's charges, and show the reader thereby that Gene still does not have full knowledge of what happened when Finny fell from the tree. To preserve in the reader's mind the image of Brinker as a threat, Knowles has the boys playfully dub him Madame Chiang Kai-shek, or "Yellow Peril." Brinker has been instrumental all along in creating nicknames for the other boys; now at last they have named him. Fittingly he is the great Chinese enemy and represents "peril," particularly to Gene. Thus Knowles' technique seems well suited to the task.

PURPOSE OF THE CHAPTER

Each of Knowles' chapters reminds and introduces, and Chapter Eight is a case in point. We have a strong reminder of Brinker's hostility toward Gene, of Finny's new dependence on Gene, of Gene's admiration of Finny's semi-magical powers and ideas, and of Finny's suffering since the accident. That Finny is said to have "suffered" is in itself a reminder of the entire accident. In other words, almost everything which has preceded the chapter is recalled, either by suggestion or by direct statement. This is central to Knowles' method as a novelist; it takes meticulous planning to remind the reader continuously of what has already developed. The result is of course our participation in an atmosphere of mounting suspense. As we weigh new events against old ideas - such as Brinker's new taunt against his earlier stated theory, or Finny's feelings about war against his summertime passion for war games - we become involved in the action and the meaning of the story.

At the same time as Knowles recapitulates the **themes** and events of the past narrative, he introduces new ones. Thus we find Gene racing around in a circle in preparation for the Olympics; we learn of Finny's new theory of war; we hear a new nickname for Brinker; and we hear of a change in faculty policy towards the war and the boys' responsibilities. In short, then, new information is presented against the ever-suggested background of what has passed. The chapter summarizes and initiates, recapitulates and introduces. And this is the method of narration which we observe in every chapter. But Chapter Eight seems to be a striking example of the way in which each chapter contributes to the total story. The process of adding new material to remembered old material heightens Gene's anxiety, his sense of guilt regarding Finny's fall, and his inability to evaluate both himself and Finny in any final way. Brinker becomes an even greater threat and looms imminently in the background as the story progresses. We are made to feel certain that his cruelty will burst forth sooner or later as the story progresses. The chapter seems to represent a turning point, in that it places Finny's accident against the contrasting background of the new theory about war which he expounds. We cannot help but remember that he was up in the tree originally only because of his positive feelings about the war. Thus there is a brilliant inconsistency between those feelings and the new ones he claims which causes us to doubt that he really feels so negatively about war. The artificiality of his motives is so plain that we, like Gene, simply do not know whether to take him seriously or not.

CHAPTER NINE

It is January and the boys have returned from Christmas vacation. Finny continues to entrance Gene into agreeing on a private peace, but this peace is suddenly disturbed. A recruiter from the Army ski troops comes to Devon and shows movies. Leper Lepellier, who is almost eighteen, enlists in the ski troops, thereby becoming "Devon School's first recruit to World War II," the first "liaison" between the boys at Devon and the great war on the outside. Gene's initial reaction is that the war must be unreal, for no real war could have induced the peaceful, nature-loving Leper to enlist. In any case, Leper is the only representative the boys have in the war and they jokingly imagine that he is responsible for every Allied success all over the world. At the same time, Leper's enlistment causes the other boys to search their own hearts as they try to decide whether they are courageous or afraid.

Finny in the meantime continues to draw Gene into a private world inhabited by just the two of them. While the general enthusiasm of the boys wanes, Finny comes up with plans for a Winter Carnival. There is a ski-jumping contest, prizes, judges, and even, by Finny's request, a torch carrier from Olympus to open the games. The Winter Carnival is Finny's self-styled Olympics, and he enters Gene in the decathlon event. All in all, Finny establishes a separate peace for the boys and Devon. This peace is abruptly shattered when a telegram arrives from Leper, who has escaped and needs help. The boys are forced to realize that war - in the form of Leper's unhappiness - has broken in upon them at last in a real and important way. Leper's telegram thus brings to a close a major portion of the book.

Comment: Leper's Enlistment

When Leper Lepellier enlists in the army ski corps, Devon becomes attached to the war. Leper is the first real link between the boys and the war which they have been reading about. Leper's decision to enter is actually fairly logical. In the first place, he is not quite eighteen years old. Thus if he enlists he can chose his own corps, as opposed to being placed anywhere once he becomes eighteen. Furthermore, Leper has always liked to ski. Earlier in the story we found Leper out on skis going cross-country and taking pictures of nature. Finally, as a naturalist, Leper feels that there is a certain evolution taking place of which he is a significant part. Those who had started to race on skis must have been working toward the role that men on skis might play in the war. Military skiing evolves out of skiing for pleasure. Leper explains that the house fly would have become extinct if it had not developed fast reflexes; so too, he explains logically, would skiing become extinct if it were not for wartime ski racing.

It is appropriate that Leper should be the first to enlist. Brinker Hadley had always been the one to talk the most about enlisting. His reaction to Leper's enlistment is to minimize his civilian existence. While he is not actually enlisting himself, he at least must reduce his nonmilitary aspects. There is a kind of horror in Leper's enlistment which is best suggested by Gene's inability to think about it seriously. It seems almost inconceivable that the quiet, shy, sensitive "naturalist" Leper should be the first to go to war. Thus when Leper leaves, "for a few days the war was more unimaginable than ever." The only way the boys are able to discuss Leper is through comic speculation regarding his role in Allied assaults. Thus when it is reported that an attempt has been made upon Hitler's life, the boys can jokingly imagine that the would-be assassin was

Leper. In other words, they are unable to bring themselves to an acceptance of the fact of Leper's enlistment, even though he is their first real link to the war.

CONTINUING FINNY'S VISION OF PEACE

That Leper is chosen is so unreal that Gene is not able to deviate in any significant way from Finny's theory about the war. Gene feels that the war still has nothing to do with life at Devon; the point is brought out in the opening paragraph of the chapter.

That Leper's enlistment does not cause Finny to change his ideas becomes evident when he creates the Winter Carnival. The ironic contrast is inescapable: Leper goes off to risk his life, so Finny invents a game. The war must be kept separate from the peace at Devon. The war must not be acknowledged, in spite of the fact that Leper is going off to join in it, for Finny cannot feel abandoned. His Winter Carnival is a challenge to the war. It is created out of defiance and its effect can only be illusory. When the telegram from Leper arrives, Finny first suggests that it is a telegram for Gene from the Olympic Committee. When they realize that it is from Leper, they also realize that they cannot continue to ignore the war.

The Winter Carnival

It is important to realize that the Winter Carnival represents not only Finny's defiance of the war on the outside, but his creation of war on the inside. The Winter Carnival, like jumping from the tree and blitzball, is a large war game. Thus when Brinker begins to suggest orderly conduct, Finny has him tackled by the entire circle of surrounding boys. The result is a state of anarchy, of competition and vigorous challenge - in short, a resurgence of the wartime psychology which prevailed during Finny's earlier creations. Thus the carnival not only serves as a means by which Finny can force Gene into athletic superiority (and Gene is Finny's representative in this respect), but serves as well as a means by which Finny can supplant the rumored real war by a new, fictitious one.

Style

The reader should continue to observe the way in which Knowles includes wartime words and adjectives in almost all kinds of descriptions. A good example is provided by the statement, "The Saturday was battleship gray." By describing the gray appearance of the day in this way, Knowles delicately reinforces the atmosphere of war which is in the background at every minute. When the cider is positioned, Brinker's roommate - Brownie Perkins - is "stationed" by the jugs and told "to guard them with his life." When the fighting breaks out, Knowles writes, "the carnival's breaking apart into a riot hung like a bomb between us." The **simile** of the bomb, as the use of "battleship gray," reminds us of the idea of war. We are never allowed to escape from the implications of wartime words; instead they force us continually to consider war.

Separate Peace

Leper's telegram - with the implication of his misery and A.W.O.L. condition - ushers in the reality of war and thereby shatters the peace implied in the illusory Olympics of the Winter Carnival. The statement from which the title is taken comes at the end of the chapter when Gene explains why he tried to do his best in the Carnival games. Gene says that he and the others have been enjoying a "separate peace" in the seclusion of the Devon School. While Leper's enlistment fails to dissolve that peace, his telegram arrives to shatter it. For the boys can sense something tragic in Leper's telegram; this tragedy is suggested in Finny's face as he reads the telegram - his face passes "through all the gradations between uproariousness and shock." The word "shock" is central in our understanding of the way in which the reality of war is at last bursting forth into the private and illusory peace at Devon; shock suggests the unexpected, which in turn implies that Finny was beginning to think he could in fact prevent the war and all its horrors from intruding into Devon. In any case, Leper's telegram announces that the "separate peace" is now over, and thus the second large section of the book comes to an end.

CHAPTER TEN

The chapter opens in the present, with Gene recollecting preparations for war undertaken by himself and others his age. Most of his time in the army was exhausted in traveling around aimlessly to different places until the war was suddenly and prematurely brought to a halt by the dropping of the atomic bomb. He recalls this experience en route to Leper's house in northern Vermont, and the scene switches to the past again. As he travels, Gene hopes that Leper has not been cowardly, has had, in effect, a legitimate reason for "escaping" from the army.

When Gene arrives he meets Leper in the dining room, Leper's new favorite place. The sensitive, nature-loving Leper has been hurt badly by his experiences in the army, and in his unhappiness accuses Gene of thinking him "psycho." Leper goes on to explain that the army had planned to give him a "Section Eight" discharge, that designed for "the nuts in the service, the psychos." In further anger, Leper defensively says that Gene is "savage underneath," and then supports this view by citing the way in which Gene knocked Finny out of the tree and "crippled him for life." Gene reacts angrily but their fracas is ended when Leper's mother enters. They have lunch together and then Gene and Leper take a walk in the country. Leper recalls some of the aspects of military life - mess hall, basic training, boot camp, etc. - and explains how after a while "everything began to be inside out." Gene screams that he doesn't care about what Leper is saying because it has nothing to do with him.

Comment: Recalling The End Of The War

Gene's remarks in the opening of Chapter Ten aptly summarize the way in which the war ended before anyone thought that it would. It had always been assumed - and was assumed right down to the very end - that Gene and most of the other boys his age would die on foreign battlefields. The entire country held this view. When America dropped the atomic bomb and brought the war to a sudden and unexpected end, all of the boys Gene's age found themselves unexpectedly returned to civilian life. In a way they felt guilty, but mostly they did not feel anything. Having prepared themselves for death, they suddenly were "sentenced" to live. This "premature" termination of World War II reflects the **irony** of the boys' anticipation of war while at Devon. We have seen the way in which the boys consciously and unconsciously moved toward the reality of war-ironically only to discover that the war was over. There is an implied tragedy: those who enlisted before they were drafted were the ones to suffer. And Leper is the case in point.

Leper's "Escape"

Leper has gone A.W.O.L. for private reasons. To him the army was nothing but an oppressive horror, filled with incredible suggestions of ignorance and cruelty. Having prepared for war by taking solitary walks in the woods, Leper had never really prepared at all. When he enlisted we sensed forthcoming doom; now we see that doom in its actuality. For Leper to function successfully as a training soldier would have been impossible; placed in an insensitive world, sensitive creatures must necessarily be frustrated and defeated. What Leper has seen is so far beyond his comprehension that everything seems to be upside down and inside out. In response, he patterned his daily life in an inverted way; this was his system of compensating for the army's inversions. If their values were distorted, his actions would also be distorted. Others would eat in the mess hall and sleep in beds, but Leper could do neither. Brooms turn into men's legs and a man's face begins to look like that of a woman; in short, Leper's basic ability to view life has been damaged. The army has ruined him.

Leper As A "Psycho"

Leper's extreme reaction to the irrational aspects of the army can only seem peculiar to other people in the army. He is considered incapable of adjusting to daily army life, much less to war, and therefore will be discharged under Section Eight for "psychos" and "nuts." Knowles is of course implying that Leper is the only one in his army group who is sane; all the rest of them are actually sick. The **irony** is embodied in the concept of discharging Leper as crazy when he alone has superior wisdom. At the same time, however, there is the inescapable fact of Leper's unhappiness and inability to "fit" into the patterns of army life.

The possibility that Leper is actually sick terrifies Gene, for it forces him to meet head-on the reality of war. Leper is the one link between Devon and the war on the outside; if Leper is being destroyed, then all of the other boys can look forward only to being destroyed. If Leper's vision is distorted, then theirs will be too. If Leper is considered "psycho," there is little hope for the boys at Devon. Leper therefore carries home their shared fate.

Symbolism Of Leper's Dining Room

Leper's newly discovered preference for the dining room is symbolic of his desire for order. Life in the army has been chaotic and unpredictable; Leper explains that in the dining room there will always be three meals a day, war or peace. The dining room thus is symbolic of the entire "shelter" in which Leper is hiding from the army. He has left the army without permission but here it does not matter.

Leper's Accusation Of Gene

When Leper angrily asserts that Gene had knocked Phineas out of the tree, that Gene alone was responsible for the fact of Finny's crippled state, the book takes on a new direction. Until this point, only the bitter and cruel Brinker Hadley has implied that Gene is to blame for Finny's fall. Thus Leper's comment comes as a great shock and Gene reacts defensively - as he had, we recall, when first accused by Brinker.

Leper's accusation aptly anticipates the next chapter. For in Chapter Eleven Gene is placed on trial in connection with Finny's fall and Leper is brought in as a key witness to the crime; that Leper is already suggesting Gene's responsibility now, before the trial has been devised, makes his surprise appearance in the next chapter even more exciting. Knowles once again is carefully **foreshadowing** his own next move; he always knows exactly where he is heading and arranges small details which anticipate and magnify later happenings. Leper's accusation therefore is introduced in a timely and very significant way, looking forward expertly to developments ahead in Chapter Eleven.

When Leper accuses Gene, he suggests that Gene is "savage underneath." This suggestion, in turn, terrifies Gene because he realizes that he still does not know himself; it may just be possible that he has a real capacity for cruelty hidden "underneath" somewhere. All of his own doubts and guilty feelings are thus fortified by Leper's suggestion of hidden savage instincts, and he will be that much more nervous and uncomfortable at the forthcoming trial.

Importance Of The Chapter

Knowles accomplishes a great deal in Chapter Ten. He shows the way in which the war ended prematurely and thus had no effect on most boys, but at the same time, through the example of Leper, shows that the war did in fact have its effects on some boys. That Leper is unfit to live in a peaceful world because of his misery in the army suggests that wars, even when theoretically "ended," survive either through their effects or through one's memory of war experiences. Thus while the war ended suddenly, it did not end at all. The chapter also heightens Gene's anxieties and doubts in a very provocative way. Now Gene has been accused by someone other than Brinker; now he indeed has more to worry about than before. He is brought to the edge of his greatest fears immediately prior to his trial at Devon. Finally, again through the distortion of Leper's vision, Knowles is able to demonstrate graphically the idiocy and inherent defects of war and of army life. The reality of the war is to be brought home to Devon through the example of Leper; even Finny, in the following chapter, will admit that Leper's case has proved to him that the war really does exist. The reality of the war is presented at last, and the boys cannot escape it any longer.

A SEPARATE PEACE

CHAPTER ELEVEN

When he returns to Devon, Gene finds Finny actively engaged in a snowball fight which he of course had organized. Finny "recruits" Gene onto his team, and at the same time he inquires about Leper. The snowball fight rages on as a war game, and Gene explains that Leper has gone A.W.O.L. Brinker guesses that Leper must have been scared and "cracked up," but himself is momentarily crushed when Gene informs him that this guess was correct. Finny is also sobered; while he says that there is no war, it is clear that he knows that the war really does exist.

Life at Devon becomes increasingly pervaded by the reality of the war and officer-training programs are described daily in the school chapel. In the meantime, Brinker takes Gene aside and tells him to stop pitying Finny because Finny will start pitying himself. Brinker points out in a malicious and ambiguous fashion that it would be good for Gene if everyone could forget about Finny's accident.

Back in their room, the boys study Caesar's war commentaries together. Finny confesses to Gene that he is now convinced that the war is real, and also explains that he has seen Leper hiding in various places around the school grounds. Later, Brinker and three friends come to the room and take Finny and Gene to the First Building where they find ten seniors dressed in black gowns and sitting on a platform like a tribunal. Brinker is conducting a war trial, investigating the cause of Finny's accident and ambiguously accusing Gene as the guilty party. Finny is a war casualty (as is Leper) and the country, Brinker asserts, demands an inquiry and explanation. Brinker asks Finny to recall the events leading up to his actual fall and slowly it becomes evident that Gene was up on the branch with Finny (Finny had first thought Gene was on the ground); to everyone's surprise, Finny tells the assembled boys that Leper is on school grounds. Leper is brought to the trial as a key witness who had been present when the accident occurred. Leper says he had seen both boys in the tree, looking "as black as death" against the bright sun behind them. Finny ends the trial by rising angrily, cursing at Brinker, and for the first time starting to cry.

Comment: The Chapter As A Climax

Chapter Eleven is the **climax** of the story. Not since Finny's actual fall has the tone and action of the book been as important to our understanding. We have participated in Gene's growing doubts and in Finny's refusal to blame Gene in any way for what had happened. Now at last the air is cleared: Brinker is directly accusing Gene of a criminal act, just as Leper had in the previous chapter. The entire scene is somber. The picture of the ten other boys gathered together in black gowns to sit in judgment of Gene is a terrifying one. For Finny, who cares for no one and nothing except Gene, the possibility that Gene was responsible for his fall is shattering. When Finny cries for the first time, the book reaches a sharp **climax** that can only produce a generalized atmosphere of gloom and unhappiness, appropriate now that the boys have accepted war as a reality.

Finny's Recognition Of The War

Early in this chapter, Gene begins to recapitulate Finny's theory of the war, hoping that Finny will join in the discourse as he always has. But this time Finny merely smiles half-heartedly and says, "Sure, There isn't any war." But even Finny, the master architect of fantasies, the master planner of illusions which would prevent the war from becoming a reality, is no longer able to persist in his illusion. He is openly recognizing the war for what it is. We recall that when Chapter Ten closed, Gene violently told Leper to stop talking about the war and about his experiences. For Gene it was painful to recognize the reality of the war announced by Leper's private tragedy. Now, we find Finny going through the same kind of personal agony but finally making the only possible conclusion: the war is real. Finny explains to Gene that Leper's example has forced him to recognize the war.

Finny goes on to explain that he knew the war was real when he saw Leper sneaking around in the bushes. Seeing Leper crazy is, in effect, seeing the war. When Finny reiterates his recognition of the war, Gene replies, "Yes, I guess, it's a real war all right. But I liked yours a lot better." That is, Gene says that he knows very well that Finny has tried to invent another kind of war, one which could be fun, for the boys at Devon. We can recall that when the chapter began, Gene discovered Finny involved in the snowball fight and Knowles writes: "I found Finny besides the woods playing and fighting - the two were approximately the same thing to him." The equation between war and play has been forming through Finny's activities throughout the book. The final stage of that process was the suggestion that an illusory Olympics would stand for the large war. But in any case, Finny's final and total recognition of the war arrives in the climactic Chapter Eleven.

The Last War Game

The snowball fight is, in effect, the last of Finny's war games. And, as in the Winter Carnival, the final result is anarchy. Gene is "recruited" by Finny to be on his team; they become "allies"; Brinker has "a sense of generalship" which becomes lost. People switch teams; there is betrayal and loyalty, attack and retreat. But the fight ends in the only way possible: all the boys turn on Phineas and bombard him heavily with snow balls until he has obviously been defeated. This game, representative of all his games, ends in his final defeat. The symbolism is apparent: with Finny's recognition of the war, his illusory and entertaining war-play creation must end. The snowball fight becomes the symbol of the last bit of "separate peace" at Devon.

The Inscription Over The Door

Over the main door of the Devon School's First Building, where Finny and Gene are taken by Brinker and his three friends to be interrogated, is the Latin inscription, "Here Boys Come to Be Made Men." While it is possible to interpret this as obviously symbolic, signaling the fact that the trial will cause Finny, Gene and the others to re-evaluate themselves and then mysteriously grow up to maturity, it seems more likely that Knowles has included the inscription as a kind of sad **irony**. The inscription probably suggests different reasons for maturity than those which seem truly operative. A Boy doesn't really come to be a Man through the simple process of education in the First Building; rather, the boys grow to maturity by way of terrifying and highly personal interactions with each other through which anxieties are both created and calmed. The turbulent world created by Brinker's accusations and cold, forthright hostility is one which demands that a boy, to survive, must become a man. Particularly in a time of war, and particularly in light of the boys' respect for bravery, becoming a man in as necessary as it is not inevitable. Self-control and resolution must be pursued consciously.

The Trial: Groping Towards The Truth

Brinker is a relentless trial lawyer in the somber scene in the First Building. Brinker is not even certain about Finny's accident, but he is willing to keep guessing, keep suggesting with calculated malice, that Gene is in some way responsible for what happened to Finny. Brinker is of course strengthened in this belief by Gene's original and still existing fear over the entire matter. Brinker's original charge had triggered Gene's self-doubts and belief in his guilt. We recall how several times Gene went independently to Finny to confess this guilt, although Finny refused to believe him.

In the trial, Brinker leads the discussion slowly towards the truth. Finny explains that he was in the tree, but that Gene was on the ground. Then he realizes that Gene also was in the tree. Gene first thinks he was down at the bottom of the tree, climbing up on the rungs. Then Leper arrives and clearly remembers that he saw two boys on the branch and then a pistonlike movement in which the boy nearest the trunk dipped and the one on the end of the branch fell. This is as far as the truth goes. Whether Gene jounced the branch and caused Finny to fall, or whether Finny lost balance and caused Gene to dip slightly cannot be known. But Brinker is interested not only in the truth; he wants to destroy an enemy for he is at war. In his insensitive manner, Brinker never once considers the effects which his accusations of Gene might have on Finny. He has made Gene the enemy and is determined to be victorious.

Saturated With War

From beginning to end, from snowball fight to trial, Chapter Eleven is saturated with war. Everything is part of the war. For example, we can consider the hunted, ferocious tone of Leper's statement toward the end of the trial when he says that he is not going to implicate himself. Leper is part prisoner-of-war and part chief witness at a war trial, but no matter where he places the emphasis, there is no doubt that for him everything that he says and does derives its meaning from the horror of the war.

Knowles continues to use the language of war in his descriptions. Gene wonders to himself what the "uniform" will be next spring - khakis, suntans, etc. A snowball can become "treacherous," loyalties can become "entangled," and friends "allies." Then there is the underscoring of war when the boys are describing their reading of Caesar's accounts of war and their discussion of a "surprise attack." This reading, the small explosive fight in Leper's dining room, and Finny's tears, along with virtually everything in the chapter, heighten our awareness of the reality of war.

Peace To The North

Throughout the book there are occasional guesses regarding what might exist all the way up at the end of the woods on the northern side of Devon. Whenever life at Devon begins to seem more oppressive, Gene speculates that there must be a beautiful and peaceful place, an untouched grove of trees, somewhere up to the north. It is appropriate that we find Gene thinking about this imagined peaceful place in Chapter Eleven, which has its explosive war trial. This peaceful place to the north exists only in the imagination. Everyone is able to imagine a utopia of one sort or another. To Gene, besieged on all sides by military matters, Brinker's hostility, Leper's psychological problems, Finny's ambiguity, and invitations to join officer-training programs, it is only natural that he turn in his imagination to a better world, a world where there would be only lovely dark trees and no newsreels about war in Europe.

Finny's Second Fall

At the very end of Chapter Eleven, after Brinker has accused Gene of being responsible for Finny's fall from the tree, Finny rushes out of the room crying and seconds later they hear him go crashing down the white marble stairs of the First Building. Finny has had another "accident" and this time there can be no doubt that this is all it was - in a technical sense. But on the other hand, all of the boys trying to fix blame for the first fall have inadvertently caused this second fall. For if they had not upset Finny so badly, or even brought him to the First Building that night at all, he never could have fallen. Cruelty has now definitely led to disaster; in his desire to destroy Gene, to fix him as the one to blame, Brinker is now largely responsible for Finny's second and greater fall. We have come a full circle.

Ironically - and tragically - what was probably an accident has slowly led to something which is not quite an accident, something which could not have happened if it were not for the first accident. Without Finny's first fall, there could have been no trial of investigation; and without a trial of investigation to provoke Finny to run hastily and clumsily, with his cane, out of the room toward the stairs, there could have been no second fall. Thus we have traveled with Knowles and the boys at Devon in a cruel and vicious circle, one appropriate to the wartime atmosphere dominating American life, and one whose circumference has included all aspects of life at Devon. Separate peace has led to separate disaster; private fun has finally been transformed into private terror. The great peaceful woods to the north remain unknown.

CHAPTER TWELVE

Phil Latham, the wrestling coach, is brought to the scene of the accident and makes Finny lie still until Dr. Stanpole arrives. Many students gather around the marble staircase and then lift Finny away in a chair; to Gene he seems like "some tragic and exalted personage, a stricken pontiff." Finny's leg has a clean break this time.

Mr. Ludsbury orders Gene to go to his room, but instead Gene sneaks around to the infirmary where Finny will be taken. For a short time Gene is all alone, crouched on the ground and on the brink of despair, busily imagining nonsensical things. Finny arrives in Dr. Stanpole's car and is taken into the infirmary. Gene talks to him through the window, explaining that he wants to help, but Finny remains angry and unreceptive. Gene, driven into further introspection, imagines that he has only existed like a dream in a curious world, and heads for the school stadium.

In the morning Gene awakes underneath the stadium stands and returns to his room where he finds a note from Dr. Stanpole requesting that Finny's things be brought to the infirmary. Once there, Finny still is unreceptive. As he listens to Gene talk, however, Finny finally admits Gene's innocence. Finny knows that Gene did not try to hurt him on purpose. Finny cannot help feeling very unhappy, though, for he knows that his leg injury will prevent him from participating in the war, and now, as always, Finny wants desperately to be in the war, even though Gene correctly tells him he would not be any good in a war because, for example, he is always changing sides.

Gene wanders around aimlessly and later meets Dr. Stanpole who begins by saying, "This is something I think boys of your generation are going to see a lot of," and then announces that Finny is dead. Dr. Stanpole loses control of himself as he tries to explain that some marrow from the broken bone must have been released into the blood stream and gone to the heart, killing Finny immediately.

Comment: Gene As An Extension Of Finny

Throughout the novel there are references to the ways in which Gene feels as if he were an extension of Finny. After the original accident, we recall, Finny as much as told Gene that he was to do things now for both of them. We remember in particular how angry Finny was when he learned that Gene was going out as assistant crew manager. Now, following the second fall, Gene cannot help feeling that the accident has happened to himself as well as to Finny. When Finny is carried away in a chair, it seems logical to Gene that he himself should have been one of the boys carrying it. Gene would have become, in effect, one of Finny's legs, because "Phineas had thought of me as an extension of himself." When Gene recalls attending Finny's funeral later on, he explains that he "could not escape a feeling that this was my own funeral." And by viewing himself as an extension of Finny, Gene has failed to see other truths about himself and other truths about Finny; thus, immediately after this second accident, Gene has "the desolating sense of having all along ignored what was finest in him". When Finny dies, it follows that a part of Gene must also die, in light of the notion of Gene's being an extension of Finny which has been developed consistently throughout the book.

Gene's Dream World

The horrible reality of Finny's accident forces Gene to recognize the bitterness and devastation possible in life. Until this second accident, Gene has more or less lived in an illusory world of dreams, a world symbolized by the imagined locale beyond the horizon. Leper's tragic story forced all of the boys to see the reality of war, but somehow Finny's second accident is much more frightening. That he lives in a world where such a nice person could be allowed to be struck twice by the same bolt of lightning becomes unbearable to Gene. At first he feels that his "whole life at Devon has been a dream," but then quickly changes his mind, deciding that everything at Devon was intensely real except himself. By becoming an extension of Finny, on the one hand, and by following a pattern of daily life designed to exclude unpleasant realities like war, Gene has never come to grips with the problems of his own existence. There is no escaping the similarity between this attitude and Leper's explanation of how everything seemed to be turned inside out. As one begins to be aware of the ugliness of a world turned inside out by war, one's own feelings and ideas become warped. Leper has enjoyed withdrawing into the world of nature. For similar reasons, Gene had withdrawn into a dream world established by Finny. Only when Finny has his second fall does Gene seem to admit that indeed it had been only a dream world.

Approaching The War

As the novel unfolds, we are not simply observing the war move closer to Devon; rather, we are watching boys growing older and therefore necessarily approaching the war. Leper's enlistment delivered the message: the war is real and boys at Devon will soon participate in it. Leper himself is viewed as one of two war casualties (Finny being the other), for all the boys become increasingly aware of the fact that a separate peace is simply not available and that they are moving closer to the war.

Finny's Attraction To The War

Finny's theory that the war did not exist was his defense against recognizing his own inability to participate in the war. Now, following his second accident and alone with Gene in the infirmary, Finny confesses that he wants very much to be in the war - in one way or another. He explains that he has been writing to the various branches of the United States armed forces; having been told "no soap," Finny has even written personal letters to General de Gaulle and to Chiang-Kai-shek; he is still considering writing somebody in Russia. For Finny, it has never mattered which team he was on. In the last of his war games, the snowball fight, we recall the typical way in which he easily joined the different teams, and how in "blitzball" he had even ruled out the possibility of having teams. To Finny war is attractive because it represents an opportunity for individuals to excel, to try their hardest to overcome an announced enemy. War and sports are one and the same thing to Finny; as a great athlete, he naturally assumes that the challenge of war presented to the individual competitive spirit cannot be equaled in any other aspect of life. Thus with a broken leg, Finny only feels bitter about his own inability to participate in the war. He alone, of all the boys at Devon, is not afraid of the war, mostly because he can hardly see the war as anything other than a demanding and challenging sport. Thus he shouts, "What good are you in a war with a busted leg!" When Gene politely suggests that Finny might not like being in Russia, Finny replies, "I'll hate it everywhere if I'm not in this war!" He explains, honestly, that he has created the various activities at Devon simply to shut out the war and his inability to become a significant part of it. Gene is aware of Finny's unrealistic attraction toward the war and points out that Finny would be switching teams and in general doing all sorts of crazy, unmilitary things; he aptly summarizes, "You'd make a mess, a terrible mess, Finny, out of the war."

Finny's Death

When Finny dies, one of Devon's only two war casualties has become a war death. Dr. Stanpole views Finny's death as an accident, a horrible thing that can happen, and can happen with more frequency when the country is at war. He makes it perfectly clear that Finny's death has been caused by the war's entering into certain aspects of Devon life: Finny had died because some of his bone marrow had accidentally entered his blood stream. However, there is the inescapable conclusion that he would not have been on the operating table if Brinker had not been filled with the spirit of war. So, indirectly, it remains true that the war killed Finny. Everything in the book has been building towards doom. This doom is completed through the absurd and unnecessary death of Finny.

CHAPTER THIRTEEN

As the final chapter opens, the Far Common of the Devon School is being taken over by the army. Olive drab jeeps and trucks bring in training soldiers who "occupy" the field and move into the Far Common dormitory. As Gene surveys this arrival, he realizes that no one has accused him of being responsible for what happened to Finny.

Mr. Hadley, Brinker's father, arrives at the school and lectures the boys on bravery, heroism, the importance of building a successful military career, and in general simply overflows with proud memories of his experiences in World War I. He naturally is disgusted with Gene when Gene remarks that he hopes never to see a foxhole. Brinker himself cannot accept his father's mindless announcement that everyone should be willing to die for his country.

As the conversation with Mr. Hadley goes on, Gene thinks of the uniqueness of Finny and then about the war. In the first place, he knows at last that wars are not caused - as Finny had asserted - by fat old men (like Mr. Hadley), but rather by "something ignorant in the human heart." And secondly, he knows that for him the hard part of war is over; it has been endured at Devon. For the real horror of war is slowly mitigated through the difficult period of preparation of war, not through actual war experiences. And on this note the novel ends.

Gene's Innocence

Knowles never directly establishes whether or not Gene is to blame for Finny's first accident, but the important aspect of that accident is that it has lost its relevance. Although Finny is now dead, the accident can never again acquire the kind of importance it began to have earlier, because the war itself has come to Devon. When the boys see the soldiers and trucks arriving at Devon, they know that all else - like the quarrels and accusations of schoolboys - is, by comparison, of little significance. Gene will never know exactly what happened up in the tree that summer, but he will be able to feel assured that no one is blaming him for what happened. Finny's accident will always be just that, an accident which contained horror and surprise but which nevertheless contributed to the maturation of the other boys at Devon, and particularly to Gene's.

Finny's Uniqueness

Knowles established Finny's uniqueness early in the story by demonstrating Finny's eccentric actions and ideas. Gene now realizes that Finny, and only Finny, had been able to create a nearly successful alternative to the reality of war, had been able, in effect, to prevent the reality of war and of other unpleasant aspects of life from becoming personal disaster. Each of the other boys at Devon had been overwhelmed by the war in one way or another. Each had been unable to accept the reality of the war, and their inability to do so has been exemplified primarily through the experiences of Leper. Finny is unique because he was the only boy not ready to surrender to the war as a force which must inevitably engulf him. Finny's character remained remarkably intact from beginning to end; with the strongest personality he endures the worst, right up to his ironic death. After the initial accident he easily could ignore the possibility of Gene's responsibility, for that would have been out of character. While Brinker Hadley becomes increasingly militant, and while Gene's self-doubts grow, Finny alone maintains his original, unified personality. Gene says that Finny had successfully resisted all the pressures of his home, of school, even of the war. The hostile world had tried its hardest, and nothing it could do defeated Finny. "So at last I had." The final comment underlines the uniqueness of the **irony** in Finny's death. He alone was able to cope with life, to sift the good from the mixture of good and bad, and he alone died. The horrible **irony** is that the person most fit for existence is finally denied it.

Cause Of War

It is important to grasp Knowles' view of the cause of war as he presents it in this final chapter. Throughout the book Knowles has presented Finny's theory that the war was a lie created by fat, selfish old men, and this idea has forced us to consider precisely why war does exist. While we do not accept Finny's oversimplified explanation, we nevertheless find ourselves asking, "Why must there be war at all?" Knowles offers his own explanation when Gene realizes "that wars were made instead by something ignorant in the human heart." The kind of ignorance which Gene is thinking about is exemplified by Brinker's increasingly ignorant cruelty. Brinker becomes militant to the point of idiocy as the "trial" of Gene begins to come to a **climax**. Such ignorant and overzealous behavior could easily cause a larger war somewhere else in the world. Knowles has attempted to demonstrate the very ignorance that can cause wars.

Preparing For The Enemy

One of the important **themes** to emerge in the final chapter is that preparing for wars is much harder than actually being in wars. One first faces the enemy when one accepts the fact that an enemy exists and that one will have to fight it eventually.

One's commitment to preparation for the war is, in effect, ones' first real confrontation with the enemy. Once one knows that an enemy exists, one prepares a defense. Brinker becomes more military and abandons school activities. Leper goes off by himself skiing, but then enlists. Finny unconsciously wards off the enemy by creating alternatives like The Super Suicide Society and the Olympics 1944. Quackenbush has been aggressive and mean to everyone. In other words, each boy was preparing for the enemy, consciously and unconsciously, in different ways. The final sentence of the novel aptly summarizes this defense-building process which constitutes preparations for the war: "All of them, all except Phineas, constructed at infinite cost to themselves these Maginot Lines against this enemy they thought they saw across the frontier, this enemy who never attacked that way - if he ever attacked at all; if he was indeed the enemy."

The Final Chapter's Importance

Chapter Thirteen does very little to advance the story in the sense of providing new action. Nothing "happens"; the Devon School simply undergoes the final transformation into a wartime place. When the trucks, jeeps, troops, and even Mr. Hadley, all arrive, life at Devon has been given its final breath. Now everything will be secondary to the national war effort. The final chapter brings the novel to a close, to borrow T. S. Eliot's phrase, "not with a bang, but a whimper." Knowles presents his explanation of the cause of war, and, more importantly, explains the theory behind the novel: that each boy must face his own enemy in his own way and respond with different defenses. The novel has been a war novel from start to finish and the last chapter underlines this. The peak of the action comes when Finny is reported dead. This is the culmination of everything toward which the book has been working, for Finny is no longer simply a "war casualty" in a figurative sense. He has actually died because the spirit of war has infected and saturated Devon School life. The final chapter adds nothing to the significance already given to the book through Finny's death; instead, Knowles ties together loose ends and presents certain philosophical statements which enlarge our understanding of the book. If we read through the book a second time, with Knowles' final explanations in mind, we are even more impressed by the extreme delicacy of the art with which the book was written. It is a masterpiece both in thematic significance - as a demonstration of the psychology of war - and in artistic significance - as an example of craftsmanship in the service of meaning.

A SEPARATE PEACE

CHARACTER ANALYSES

There are four principal characters in Knowles' *A Separate Peace*, and each of the four becomes involved with the other three in a variety of unusual ways; the four are: Phineas, usually called Finny (no last name), Gene Forrester, Brinker Hadley, and Edwin - "Leper" - Lepellier. Some of the less important characters are Bobby Zane and Chet Douglas, two of the boys frequently present at the various war games; Leper's mother whom we meet briefly when Gene visits Leper; Brinker's father, who visits Devon toward the end of the novel; Mr. Prud'homme, a master during the summer session; Dr. Stanpole, the doctor at Devon and the one who performs the fatal operation on Finny's leg; Cliff Quackenbush, the bully who fights with Gene at the beginning of crew practice. For the most part, the novel concentrates on the quartet of central characters and we can review them as unique individuals.

Phineas

It is important to realize that Finny's last name is never presented. Finny is just Finny; he is unique enough to exist without a last name because he is, in every respect, a unique person. Finny is a powerful character and exerts a charismatic charm over the other boys. He has always been Devon School's outstanding athlete. He has not only natural athletic coordination; he has a very strong competitive spirit and the will to win. We can recall his desire to keep secret the fact that he broke the school's swimming record; he was more interested in proving his capability to himself than to the other boys. His ability to excel in sports is of course tragically marred by his "accident," and thus he coaches Gene in the hope that Gene will be able to represent both of them in sports.

Finny is the natural leader of the other boys and is responsible for the invention of the various war games and new athletic activities designed to prove manliness such as The Super Suicide Society of the Summer Session and blitzball. It is only because of his scheming that these activities become popular and exciting.

Finny has very definite feelings about the war: to him, the war is the false creation of a bunch of fat old men who stand to prosper when the country is at war. Finny would actually like to be in the war, but after his accident he knows that it is impossible for him to participate. Thus part of his refusal to acknowledge the reality of the war is his defense against being uncomfortable about being unable to be in the war. He writes letters, we should remember, to the Russians and the Chinese, as well as to the various armed services of America, offering his help. To Finny war is really a game, another kind of sport; his confidence in his abilities to be good in war stems from his knowledge that he has always been good in sports.

From a thematic point of view, Finny represents the extreme tragedy of war. He would not have organized the Suicide Society if wartime psychology had not penetrated the atmosphere at Devon; he would not have fallen the first time if the Society had not been started; he would not have been at the trial of Gene if Brinker Hadley had not been filled with a militant spirit; and he would not have had the second fall and died if he had not been at this trial. In other words, the series of "ifs" which lead tragically to the death of Finny could not have occurred without a wartime psychology, without the newsreels, sermons in chapel, etc., all focusing attention on the war on the outside and the daily bombing missions over Central Europe.

Our view of Finny, then, must be as a tragic hero. He is heroic in the sense that he does not fear war and certainly does not fear death. He is the warrior figure, the powerful athlete destroyed by horrible coincidence and circumstance. He is virtually lionized by the other boys and leads them in a completely natural and unassuming way. He is consistently presented by Knowles, for from beginning to end he remains loyal both to his best friend Gene and to himself.

Gene Forrester

Gene is the narrator of the story, a young man returning to the Devon School and recalling his experiences there as a sixteen-year-old student in the summer of 1942 and the following year. He is quite definitely made subordinate to Finny. Gene worships Finny and wants desperately to be his "best friend"; however, occasionally it occurs to Gene that he really envies rather than loves Finny. Gene fears that perhaps unconsciously he wants to become superior to Finny and thus he feels unusually guilty after Finny falls from the tree. From this point on, Gene is plagued by self-doubts and speculates as to the true intentions underlying all his actions. For the most part, however, Gene is able to view himself instinctively as an extension of Finny; he will help Finny in his studies and he will even allow Finny a certain amount of vicarious competitive satisfaction through his training for the imaginary Olympics. Before the accident we see that Gene and Finny are very close; for example, they both cajole each other into breaking the rules on the very first day of the summer session.

In all respects, Gene Forrester is secondary to Finny. Gene almost serves as a biographer recalling the greatness of someone else. While Gene allows us certain insights into his own mind, he nevertheless directs our attention toward the image of himself as Finny's champion and defender. This image is sharpened dramatically when Gene fights with Cliff Quackenbush who had unknowingly and indirectly insulted the absent, crippled Finny. Gene knows himself well enough to realize that he is merely a part of Finny rather than a completely separate person. Gene's imagination is inferior to that of Finny, although Gene is able to think about life at Devon in a more comprehensive way. This is sensible, for Gene after all is the narrator and Knowles must not let too much attention be directed to him; Finny is the unique character in the novel and Gene is in the book both to tell the story and to magnify Finny's uniqueness.

Brinker Hadley

Brinker is the most aggressive boy at Devon. He has long been the leader in extracurricular activities and school politics. He is not in direct competition with anybody else at Devon, for he knows that Gene is a better student and that Finny is the school's best athlete. Brinker's main motivation is to live up to his father's image of him. Mr. Hadley is a war veteran and therefore filled with the idea that war is an important and patriotic experience which all young men should have.

As the war on the outside spreads, Brinker withdraws into a private world. He begins to stop going to school activities, and he starts wearing khaki-colored clothes and talking like a soldier. He becomes, as it were, Devon's soldier-in-residence. It is vitally important to him to assume the characteristics of an aggressive and brave soldier. And thus he begins to badger the nervous Gene. Brinker's early flirtation with the military image becomes an overpowering aspect of his entire constitution. He becomes aggressive and makes absolutely no effort to hide his hostility. Thus he attacks Gene, forcing him into the trial situation as if it were a trial of a horrible war crime; he says that the country demands an explanation of Finny's casualty and he, Brinker, is going to give the country that explanation. While we easily see Brinker's hostility we do not really understand it until his father arrives at Devon; Knowles might have improved the characterization of Brinker by introducing something of the nature of the relationship between Brinker and his father earlier in the book.

In any case, Brinker never becomes as important a character as either Finny or Gene. Brinker is more of a type than an individual. As a natural debater and politician he brings on disaster when he attacks Gene's vulnerable feelings of self-condemnation.

Leper Lepellier

Leper is the shy, sensitive boy who prefers moody isolation to active participation. He is a "loner" and enjoys going off by himself on walks in the woods where he takes photographs of beaver dams. He is the school naturalist and, being shy, is only able to join with the other boys after careful consideration of external prompting.

Thematically, Leper is the one real link between the boys at Devon and the real war on the outside. He enlists almost impulsively in the Army Ski Patrol in hopes of simply skiing in the woods. But the military training becomes too much for the sensitive Leper and he goes, in his own term, "psycho." Fearing that he will be discharged for psychological reasons, Leper goes A.W.O.L. (absent without leave) and furtively returns to his country home in the Vermont woods. Leper's inability to conform to army life turns him into the boys' first war "casualty" (Finny is the other "casualty"), and represents to them the real horror of war. Until learning of his trouble, the boys had talked about Leper in heroic terms. They imagined that he was responsible in one way or another for every major Allied victory. But when it is disclosed - through his mysterious telegram- that Leper has been defeated by the army experience, the boys can no longer imagine him in an entertaining way. Leper becomes the key symbol of the ugly reality of war; in Chapter Eleven Finny openly confesses to Gene that Leper's accident has opened his eyes; if Leper could crack up as he has, then the war must be real.

Aside from Leper's thematic importance as a link between the boys at Devon and the reality of war, he does not become as well known to us as Finny. We see Leper's outstanding characteristics - his shyness, sensitivity, and his love of nature and solitude - right from the start, and we pity him when he finds his world being turned inside out. But there is little development of Leper between our first and last views of him; true, he becomes psychologically disturbed, but nevertheless we never see into his private feelings.

The Four Main Characters In Integration

Each of the four main characters has a certain relationship to each of the others, but the special relationship in the book is that of love, trust, loyalty, and even mystery between Finny and Gene. Here is the perfect relationship established between the school student and the school athlete; the school politician and the school naturalist never reach the same dramatic importance in our minds. Finny's presence is felt almost at all times; his influence never ceases. Even when he is lying in the hospital his spirit seems ubiquitously involved in Devon life, and he is like the ghost of Hamlet's father.

Names

There is possible symbolism in the names of the four major characters but Knowles is not specific. Finny might suggest the French word "finis," meaning finished. That is, Finny is the main war casualty, the one character whose life is ended because of a world saturated with the psychology of war. Gene Forrester's name suggests the magical forests to the north, the imaginary better and more peaceful places that he describes at frequent intervals throughout the book; Brinker Hadley suggests the whole idea of "brinkmanship," of living on the "brink" of war, pushing for further war to the point beyond which would lie disaster (this term, "brinkmanship," was in vogue when the novel was written); and Leper Lepellier can be seen as an undesirable "leper," for after he goes A.W.O.L. he represents something ugly and horrible to the rest of the boys. All of these possible interpretations are purely speculative and certainly not of major importance. The student should have a firm idea in his mind of each of the four main characters and of the relationships between them; the symbolism of the names is only introduced as an intriguing possibility.

A SEPARATE PEACE

. . . .

EVALUATION

Ever since it was first published in 1960, John Knowles' *A Separate Peace* has been highly praised. While there has been no full critical study of the novel, countless reviewers have found it to be an exciting and dramatic presentation of a certain set of emotions at a crucial moment of history. The dialogue between Gene and Finny unfolds against the background of World War II, and the Devon playing fields quite literally become extensions of both American training camps and foreign battlefields. The novel has been greeted with near-unanimous praise. Knowles has written a great book, a rare story, and a minor "classic." Like *A Catcher in the Rye* and *Lord of the Flies*, Knowles' first novel presents a vision of life through the experiences of young boys. While Salinger's Holden Caulfield has become more of a stereotyped character, however, Knowles' Phineas has remained singular and inimitable. One reason that *A Separate Peace* has been consistently praised by reviewers is that Knowles is a master at characterization. Everything that Finny does - his bizarre adoption of the pink shirt, or holding his pants up with a Devon School tie used as a belt to show his approval of Allied bombing of Central Europe - connects logically to everything he says and to everything which Gene says about him. In other words, there are no loose ends, no ambiguous mumblings - and no overstatement.

KNOWLES' SUBTLETY

One of the further reasons for the book's success is Knowles' ability to state things in a subtle way. While the war is always present in the background, there are only a few places in the entire novel where Knowles allows Gene to state directly the horror and the atmosphere of the war. The entire characterization of Finny can probably only be understood by the author and by the original of Finny (we suspect, somehow, a biographical counterpart), for there is a certain subtlety about Finny and the crazy things he likes to do, a certain subtle impulsiveness, as it were, which we find charming if perhaps at times thoroughly mysterious. And yet we never seem to feel that there is anything illogical in the book; while we are occasionally surprised or confused, we are never disappointed. Knowles is aware of the importance of understatement and thus he allows the reader to connect many of the boys' war games to the real war on the outside. And even Leper's "crack-up" is presented with only the necessary amount of dramatic impact. Through his own explanation of the way everything seemed to become turned inside out, Leper is able to dramatize the absurdity of war without a booming overstatement or direct condemnation.

ARTISTRY OF A HIGH ORDER

The outstanding dimension of *A Separate Peace* is its artistry. On the level of description, every word seems well chosen.

The vocabulary of war is skillfully employed both in natural description and in the descriptions of the boys' various war games. Furthermore, the plot is planned with great deliberation. When Knowles is writing of Finny's first fall, he has in mind the second fall which will arrive toward the end of the book. And of course the way in which the book is outlined and divided by the major incidents such as the two falls, the fight with Quackenbush, Leper's enlistment, Brinker's demand for a trial, etc., is indicative of artistry of the highest order.

The technique of narration is to have an interchange at fixed intervals between a voice speaking in the past adolescent tones of Gene Forrester the student and a voice of a young man returning back to his preparatory school sometime after he has graduated and gone through the army. The shifts remind us of the author's final perspective; although we allow ourselves as readers to be swept up in the world at Devon, we cannot help reminding ourselves that this world is lost, and that our own youth is simply one more period through which we pass on our life-journey.

When we add together the meticulous results of careful narration, employment of war vocabulary, and expert, subtle methods of characterization, the total achievement is formidable. From every point of view, Knowles' first novel has a rare artistry, an artistry which even Knowles was not able to repeat in his second novel, which appeared two years later in 1962, *Morning in Antibes*.

A SEPARATE PEACE

ESSAY QUESTIONS AND ANSWERS

· ·

Question: What is the central concern of *A Separate Peace*?

Answer: Although one is inclined to magnify the novel's concern with the effects of World War II on boys about to become eligible for the draft, the central concern is with the basic adolescent set of emotions surrounding trust, confidence, and loyalty. What the awareness of war does is to serve to activate submerged emotions. For example, Brinker's aggressiveness had been effectively channeled through his eager participation in school activities and politics. The awareness of war resulted in his abandoning of these activities and his increased outward hostility toward the other boys. All boys feel competitive in varying degrees, but each boy tries to direct his energy to the location of his greatest potential talent. Finny thus has become a great athlete and feels that the is required to excel in sports; Gene, by contrast, is naturally inclined to study hard. Each boy, while pursuing individual goals, must necessarily decide upon the kind of relationship he is to enjoy with each of the other boys. The central problem in *A Separate Peace* is contained in Finny's and Gene's inability to from conclusions about each other and about themselves. Gene thinks that he is Finny's best friend - but he can never be sure. Finny hopes that Gene is his best friend - but he cannot make him be. Each tells himself as well as the other that the two of them are, in fact, best friends. And yet because of natural human defenses, each is unable to know that they are best friends. Knowles purposely magnifies Gene's central self-doubts through deliberate refusal to assign responsibility for Finny's fall from the tree. This "accident" causes Gene's problem of self-knowledge to be magnified. While he is loyal to Finny he cannot help feeling that perhaps he envies him; and while Finny implicitly trusts Gene, he cannot be sure that he should. From beginning to end Knowles carefully documents the uncertainty surrounding the emotions of trust, confidence, and loyalty; each boy's internal debate becomes part of the dramatic definition of adolescence.

Question: To what extent is Knowles' novel about the quest for personal identity?

Answer: Inasmuch as each of the major characters is attempting to determine where his loyalties lie, each is searching for his identity. Brinker's hostility replaces his earlier political facade, while Leper's sensitivity mushrooms out of proportion and makes him unfit for the experience of army life. Each of the major characters has been given an external definition and identity by the other boys. It is assumed that Finny is the class athlete, Gene the class student, Brinker the class politician, and Leper the class naturalist. The inadequacy of these externalized identities becomes obvious as the atmosphere of war heightens at Devon. As each boy is moved helplessly closer to the horrible, idiotic reality of war, his identity is challenged. For example, every boy must search his heart and try to discover whether he is brave or cowardly. The mere existence of war demands that every boy ask himself whether he is suited for war, whether he can acclimate himself to the rigor and cruelty of war. Since no one who has never experienced war can know how he will perform in war, each boy guesses and in so doing is groping towards identity and self-knowledge. Human relationships are either cemented or weakened when the participants discover the truth about themselves. Gene and Finny realize their mutual dependency on one another, whereas Leper remains unsupported in his decision to be a "loner." Probably he was wrong to enlist as soon as he did, but by the same token, perhaps Brinker should have enlisted earlier. Brinker is fierce because he feels that his real identity should contain the element of ferocity; he acts in a hostile manner only because he feels he ought to. Finny allows no idleness in his life for he feels that his identity depends on his ability to disassociate himself from the fact of his accident. His identity as the school athlete is shattered when he falls. And Gene's identity as Finny's best friend is weakened when he imagines that he is to blame for Finny's fall. In other words, the events of the book force each character, in different ways, to grope toward a new and firm identity. Particularly in times of war, when human beings are shuffled around in masses, does it become extremely important to preserve the value and significance of the individual human spirit. Leper's outcome contains the **theme** that war violates the individual and at the same time underlines the novel's constant concern with the individual establishment of identity.

Question: How does Knowles dramatize the war?

Answer: Knowles effectively dramatizes the war through a variety of techniques. Perhaps the most vivid method is his reference to the boys' shared preoccupation with newsreels and pictures in newspapers. In the summer of 1942 and 1943 the news media were filled with graphic depictions of suffering soldiers; reference to these media therefore automatically dramatizes the war. A second and more pervasive method of dramatization is the invention of the various games directed by Finny. Blitzball provides a very dramatic means for depicting the inherent warrior instincts; as Finny proclaims during the first attempt at blitzball, "since we're all enemies, we can and we will turn on each other all the time." The point is simple: in war there can be no "knowns," no final alliances, and no unbreakable bonds of loyalty. The chief aspect of war is reliance on individual courage and fortitude and the same reliance is also important to any success in the boys' games. Jumping from the tree is a symbol of proving military fitness, just as the fight the boys have at the Winter Olympics illustrates their willingness to dissolve all ties and turn impulsively on one of their own, in this case on Brinker Hadley.

Perhaps the greatest dramatization of the war is provided by the climactic trial scene where we see Brinker conducting what for him is a war trial. The boys sit in black gowns like a military tribunal judging a traitor. The atmosphere of war pervades the room and we sense Finny's sudden temporary disillusionment - typical of the war experience. The panic in which he leaves the room leads swiftly to his death, and the horror of war is brought home with great dramatic force.

As final key dramatizations of the war one should note Gene's fight with Cliff Quackenbush, and Leper's illegal departure from army training. In the fight at crew practice we see the drama of impulsive loyalty, a mainspring in all military endeavor. That is, even though Gene doubts his loyalty to Finny, when the situation seems to threaten Finny, Gene impulsively defends him. This sudden and uncalculated self-sacrifice lies at the heart of the war experience. And in Leper we are presented with the psychological discomfort which must become an inevitable part of the experience of war by many boys, particularly all of the quiet, shy, and sensitive boys like Leper. Through Leper's mental deterioration and loss of self-esteem, Knowles dramatizes the opposite of Gene's impulsive heroism and Finny's native courage.

Question: Is there the suggestion of a universal "separate peace"?

Answer: Yes, Knowles is careful to give Devon a certain universality which becomes increasingly present as the novel advances. The boys at Devon consciously and unconsciously attempt to establish a private world of peace safely removed from the dangerous world of war on the outside. And Knowles suggests indirectly that many boys in many schools throughout the country were busily securing such a separate peace for themselves in the summer of 1942 and in 1943. With an inevitable enlistment or conscription awaiting them, the boys quite naturally were concerned with having a last portion of peaceful life, and they were supported in this by the masters at preparatory schools who romanticized the sixteen-year-olds as the last happy and innocent Americans, the ones not yet damaged by the reality of war. Thus it is not simply a question of the boys' desiring peace, but of the adult world's desiring peace for them. It was a universal desire of the country to have some of its people undisturbed by the war.

Question: In what way are Finny and Leper similar?

Answer: Although Finny is closest to Gene, and although Finny and Gene are the dominant characters in *A Separate Peace*, we should not lose sight of the fact that Finny and Leper are the two war "casualties" and as such have something in common. Through fate (coincidence) and error (misjudgment), both Finny and Leper are brought to disaster. Leper was of course wrong to think he could endure the discipline and regimentation of army training, but he had of course idealized the experience in anticipation and sincerely thought he would spend most of his time skiing ("touring") in the woods as he always had, both at his home in Vermont and at Devon. Thus it is not really his "fault" that he cracks up, that he buckles under the strain and fears he is going "psycho." Similarly, Finny is not really at "fault" when he falls from the tree. He sincerely believes that there is a risk involved in jumping but he also sincerely believes that because of his superior athletic prowess it is unlikely that anything can happen to him. Furthermore, Finny's fate is bound up in the hostility of a militant figure, Brinker, just as Leper's fate is bound up in the suspected hostility of his superiors in army training.

While Leper's temporary insanity and withdrawal from army life suggest to the other boys, for the first time, the horror of war, Finny's death completely terminates all discussion of whether or not war is real. The silent equation in the boys' minds is that if death can be real-through the example of Finny - then war must be real. When somebody actually dies, all play-acting comes to an end. Thus both Leper and Finny as war casualties serve as illustrations of war to the other boys. Both have suffered a certain amount of psychological strain as a result of the atmosphere of war; Leper thinks everything is turning inside out, while Finny proclaims - publicly, at least-that there really is no war. Both are thus swept up by their private defense mechanisms, becoming war "casualties" in a double sense.

Question: What are the metaphorical implications of Finny's accident?

Answer: As a final consideration, we should remember that Finny's fall has symbolic overtones. On one level - the literal level of narrated action - Finny "falls" from the tree. On another level - the symbolic level of suggestion-Finny "falls" from high estate into despair. The fall is an inversion of Finny's entire world view, in the sense that he must begin to build defenses which all cripples must build. Feeling that he will be unable to participate in the war, he deliberately attempts to demonstrate his military ability. Primarily, the **metaphor** of the "fall" operates to establish Finny as a tragic hero in the full Aristotelian sense. That is, according to Aristotle's theory of tragedy, for a figure in a drama to become "tragic" he must fall from a high to a low estate. That Finny literally falls from the tree is a convenient narrative device; on the literal level it makes sense, while on the symbolic level it directs the reader's attention to the inherent tragedy of Finny's situation. The idea of injury is joined to the idea of war and Finny becomes a major piece of evidence that horrible things do happen and that war does exist. And although separate peaces may be established with some degree of success, they will never be completely separated from war because the existence of man implies the existence of war.

BIBLIOGRAPHY

BOOKS BY JOHN KNOWLES

A Separate Peace, 1960.

Morning in Antibes, 1962.

Double Vision: American Thoughts Abroad, 1964.

Indian Summer, 1966.

Phineas and Other Stories, 1968.

The Paragon, 1971.

Spreading Fires, 1974.

A Vein of Riches, 1978.

Peace Breaks Out, 1981.

CRITICISM

Ellis, James. "*A Separate Peace:* The Fall from Innocence." *English Journal,* vol. 53, no. 5, May 1964.

Halio, Jay L. "John Knowles's Short Novels." *Studies in Short Fiction,* vol. 1, no. 2, winter 1964.

Lemay, Harding. "Two Boys and a War Within." *New York Herald Tribune Book Review,* March 6, 1960.

Raven, Simon. "No Time for War." *The Spectator,* vol. 202, no. 6827, May 1, 1959.

Weber, Ronald. "Narrative Method in *A Separate Peace.*" *Studies in Short Fiction,* vol. 3, no. 1, fall 1965.

Witherington, Paul. "*A Separate Peace:* A Study in Structural Ambiguity." *English Journal,* vol. 54, no. 9, December 1965.

Wolfe, Peter. "The Impact of Knowles's *A Separate Peace.*" *University Review,* vol. 36, no. 3, March 1970.

CPSIA information can be obtained
at www.ICGtesting.com
Printed in the USA
LVHW041031170622
721528LV00014B/746

9 781645 422723